The Logistics Legends – Volume II

Real Stories. Hard Truths.
Transformational Lessons.

The Logistics Legendary Stories Continue!

Honour the superheros behind the scenes!

Disclaimer

Copyright Disclaimer © 2025 Cuilan Guo. All rights reserved. This book, including all intellectual property rights therein, is solely owned by Cuilan Guo. No part of this book may be reproduced, distributed, or transmitted in any form or by any means, including photocopying, recording, or other electronic or mechanical methods, without the prior written permission of the copyright owner, except in the case of brief quotations for review, commentary, or other non-commercial purposes as allowed by law. Unauthorized use is strictly prohibited.

Publisher Disclaimer This book is published by Signature Global Network PTY LTD. While the publisher facilitates the production, printing, and distribution of this book, all rights, ownership, and control over the content remain solely with Cuilan Guo. The publisher does not claim any ownership over the intellectual property contained within this book.

Accuracy Disclaimer While every effort has been made to ensure the accuracy and completeness of the information in this book, the authors and publisher make no representations or warranties, express or implied, about the accuracy, completeness, suitability, or availability of the content. Readers are advised to independently verify any information and consult with professionals where appropriate. The authors and publisher disclaim any responsibility for errors, omissions, or any losses, damages, or disruptions arising from reliance on this book.

Similarity Disclaimer This book is a non-fiction work and includes real-life experiences. However, names and details may have been altered to respect privacy and confidentiality, and any resemblance to persons, businesses, or incidents is coincidental unless otherwise noted with explicit consent.

Opinion Disclaimer The views, thoughts, and opinions expressed in this book belong solely to the authors and are not necessarily reflective of any affiliated organizations or entities. These opinions are based on personal experience and interpretation, and readers are encouraged to form their own views.

Explicit Content Disclaimer This book may contain explicit language, sensitive content, or themes of a mature nature. Reader discretion is advised. The content is intended for an adult audience.

Expertise Disclaimer While the authors have extensive expertise and experience in the fields discussed, this book is not intended to provide professional advice. It is meant for informational and educational purposes only. Readers should seek professional counsel for advice specific to their situation.

Ownership & Acknowledgment While the co-authors have contributed to the creation of this book through their life stories and insights, all rights, ownership, and control over this work remain solely with Cuilan Guo. Co-authors have no claim to ownership or control of the content or intellectual property, beyond what is acknowledged here.

Publisher: Signature Global Network PTY LTD

Authors: Cuilan Guo (Kristy) /Fabrizio Alvear (Pep) /Michelle Moreno/ Sam Yauner/Katharina Attana/Gavin Homer/ Monica Arce/Kalana Wickramaratne

Cover Design: Kristy Guo & Signature Global Network Creative Team

ISBN: 978-0-6456617-6-7 (paperback)
ISBN: 978-0-6456617-9-8 (E-book)

Co-Authors of *The Logistics Legends Volume II*

Cuilan Guo (Kristy)

Fabrizio Alvear (Pep)

Michelle Moreno

Sam Yauner

Katharina Attana

Gavin Homer

Monica Arce

Kalana Wickramaratne

Contents

Acknowledgements vii
Foreword ix

Chapter 1   Desire – Dare to Dream, *Rise & Shine* – by *Kristy Guo* 1
Chapter 2   From Hustle to Legacy: Lessons in Leadership and
             Growth – by *Fabrizio "Pep" Alvear* 63
Chapter 3   From Scarcity to Significance: *A Journey of Faith,
             Grit & Grace* – by *Michelle Moreno* 89
Chapter 4   Building The Leader in Me: *A journey of hard lessons
             and growth* – by *Sam Yauner* 109
Chapter 5   Becoming Me From Roots to Wings –
             by *Katharina (Kat) Attana* 139
Chapter 6   The Long Haul Building a Legacy through Purpose,
             People, and Perseverance *How a Freight Leader Navigated
             Crisis, Connection, and Change to Build a Business that
             Lasts* – by *Gavin Homer* 159
Chapter 7   The Power Within *Stories of Transformation and
             Triumph* – by *Monica Arce* 177
Chapter 8   From Struggles to Success Kalana Wickramaratne's
             Journey in Logistics – by *Kalana Wickramaratne* 193

Let's Connect 203

Acknowledgements

This book is more than a collection of stories—it's a journey of purpose, perseverance, and people. It exists because of those who walked alongside me, believed in the vision, and gave it life.

To my **beloved husband Luke**, and daughters **Sze Sze and Selena**:
Your love is my anchor. Thank you for embracing my dreams, for the joy and chaos we share, and for letting me fly while always holding me close.

To the **Signature Global Network family**:
You are not just part of a network—you are the living heartbeat of a global movement. Your trust has built a foundation where ideas turn into impact.

To my **dedicated Signature staff**:
Your loyalty, resilience, and unwavering support have carried this vision further than I ever imagined. You lead with both heart and excellence.

To **Rudee Bertie** – The Logistics Legend I proudly co-authored with:
Your belief, influence, and passion have been a driving force. Thank you for walking this journey with me from day one.

To all our **co-authors**:
Thank you for your courage to share, your commitment to this project, and your leadership in your own right. This book reflects the collective brilliance you bring to the world.

To my **C-Suite coaching clients**:
You've allowed me to witness transformation in real time. Your hunger for growth and willingness to evolve inspire me every day.

To my **church family**:
Your prayers and spiritual support have kept me centred. Thank you for reminding me of the higher calling behind all this work.

To my **friends, mentors, and supporters**:
You showed up when it mattered most. Your belief in me, especially in the unseen moments, has been a quiet but powerful light.

This book isn't just ours—it belongs to every leader, dreamer, and change-maker who believes in using their voice to shape the world.

With all my heart,
Kristy Guo

Foreword

14th October 2024, the first *Logistics Legends* book was published. That day, the book reached #1 on **Amazon** across many countries and in multiple categories.

Except for me—already an author—all seven new co-authors became well-known. Not only did they officially become international best-selling authors, but new opportunities and doors also opened for them.

When they joined the co-author program, their initial thought was the same as all the others: to **influence, empower, and inspire** the next generations. And they did! We did!

We started receiving feedback. The whole logistics industry became noisy—people started talking about the book and the individuals behind it. Testimonials poured in from LinkedIn. At global logistics conferences, there would always be someone who already knew one of us because of the book.

One of the funny feedback we received was that someone once said:

> "I thought this book was about logistics success, but it's so different—it's about the stories. Amazing stuff!"

Yes, working in one industry—no matter which one—it's easy to get absorbed in the professionalism of it all, believing everything you do should be directly related to that field. But one thing many forget is: **we are all humans.**

We may work in one industry, but we live in all industries—because we live in the same world.

When I first came up with the idea for the book, many visionaries were interested. But they were curious, cautious, overthinking. Some confirmed verbally but later backed out. Some promised to join but didn't follow through. Some said they'd consider it but never took action.

The first person who made a decision—and the fastest—was **Rudee Bertie**: a humble and successful influencer, leader, and mentor in the logistics e-commerce industry. An authentic and compassionate business investor.

We had known each other for 18 years. The last time we met in person was 10 years ago. After a quick virtual call, he simply said:

"I'm in."

When I asked why he decided so quickly, his answer was:

> "I trust you! I've seen you grow from where you were to where you are. I trust you 100%."

That sentence was short, but it carried so much weight. It gave me incredible strength.

Looking back, I now understand why so many successful CEOs who've connected with him **respect** and **appreciate** him deeply.

He is the guy.
And over time, I've realized—he is a mirror of me. That's who I am too. I've been walking this path my whole life.

To see someone who believes what you believe… who does what's right… who leads with purpose and puts **people ahead of profit**—that's something truly wonderful.

There were times when **fear and doubt** attacked me. I was aiming to find at least **20 authors**, but reality hit hard.

The more I worked toward the vision—as a believer, a visionary, and a dream-chaser—the more I discovered this truth: it's always the **10% or less** who are willing to take risks and walk a different path. That's why the mountain top is never crowded.

Nevertheless, we did it!
Eight authors in total—and that turned out to be the perfect number.

Besides **Rudee**, who is from the **United Kingdom**, we also had **Mandy Deakin-Snell**, also from the UK. Then came a remarkable group of co-authors:

- **Gilbert Ernest** from **Australia**
- **Ashwin Didwania** from the **Netherlands**, with an **Indian** background
- **Dr. Sri** from **Switzerland**, with a **Sri Lankan** background
- **Derek Scarbrough** from the **USA**
- **Deepanker Parashar** from **India**

If you haven't grabbed your copy of *Logistics Legends Volume 1* yet—**now is the time!**

Right after the book was published, I witnessed **breakthroughs and new opportunities** for all of the co-authors:

- **Gilbert** was featured on **Forbes** and offices went global after the program.
- **Rudee** was featured on magazine covers for **The World Leaders**.
- **Mandy** received more speaking invitations and more business opportunities.
- **Ashwin** was recognized at major conferences.

To name a few.
And it wasn't just career breakthroughs—it was also **family recognition**. Their family and friends started to understand more about who they truly are.

That meant everything. It was a huge moment for those who know these co-authors personally. Their families were **proud—very proud**.

I knew that feeling—because **that was where I started**.

Why *The Logistics Legends II*?

Because we've realized that the logistics industry has been **deeply underestimated** by the outside world.

There are **so many unsung heroes**—logistics superheroes—who deserve to be seen and celebrated.

As a **high-performance coach**, and with 90% of our global members and CEO clients coming from this industry, the more I listen to their stories, the more amazed I am.

These stories—real, raw, human—can **literally change lives**.

Why should you read these stories?
What can this book do for you?
How does it relate to your own journey?

Because each story in this book is **far more powerful than a popular movie**. You'll see yourself reflected in one—or many—of these journeys. You'll find moments that **resonate, inspire reflection**, and **prompt you to review your own life**.

You may even discover a new direction, a renewed purpose, or a long-lost goal.

Some stories may help you confront and heal from past wounds—giving you the space for **self-discovery and recovery**.

These co-authors didn't just share the shiny surface of success—they shared the **mess behind the success**.

The **real** stuff.

The **human** stuff.

Maybe you're at a crossroads right now—making tough life or business decisions. This book can offer you the **clarity** and perspective you need to move forward with confidence and wisdom.

And we didn't stop with just *The Logistics Legends Book*.

Five months later, we launched *The World's Thought Leaders*—and it **broke records**.

In less than three months, we printed 1,000 copies, which quickly made their way across the globe—**USA, Philippines, India, Australia, Netherlands, Germany, Singapore, Thailand**, and more.

Our co-authors began signing books at events, getting featured, and some even secured **paid speaking gigs**. Sounds unbelievable? But it's **true** and **transformative!** Because **nothing is impossible when you believe.**

Final advice:
Don't just read this book—**feel it**. Let it challenge you, inspire you, and push you to think bigger.
And if something stirs in your heart as you read—don't ignore it.
Maybe you're not just meant to be a reader…
Maybe you're meant to be the **next storyteller**.

Your story could be the one that changes someone else's life.

So read with courage. Reflect with honesty.
And never underestimate the power of your own journey.

The Real Legends Don't Wait. They Leap.
When I launched the first *Logistics Legends* book, I had one dream: to spotlight the souls behind the systems—the leaders who dared to take a leap of faith, roll up their sleeves, and build the logistics world from the inside out.

Now… we're back. And Volume 2 is louder, bolder, and even more soul-stirring.

These aren't just business stories. These are heart stories. Of first-generation entrepreneurs who built empires from scratch. Of mentors who shaped lives before they scaled companies. Of trailblazers who fought against the odds—not just for profits, but for purpose.

What unites all these legends? They didn't wait for perfect conditions. They moved. They acted. They believed—before the world did.

You're about to meet visionaries like Pep, who turned $60 million in logistics into legacy. Michelle, who brought faith to freight. Sam, who led with heart before he had industry experience. Kat, who smashed ceilings and mentored across continents. Monica, Kalana, Gavin—each one, a masterpiece of grit and grace.

These pages aren't just inspiration. They're instruction manuals for the next bold move in your business—and your life.

To every reader: this book is your permission slip to go all in. To every author: thank you for trusting me, for showing up, and for sharing your soul. You are *The Logistics Legends*.

Let's rewrite what leadership looks like.

Kristy Guo
Curator, Co-Author & Global Voice of Logistics Leadership
www.kristyguo.com | www.signaturegln.com

Chapter 1

Desire – Dare To Dream, Rise & Shine

Kristy Guo

Prologue

Hey You, I Remember You...
A Letter from Kristy—For the One Who's Ready to Remember

Hey you,
Yes, **you**.
I remember you.

You were once a pure-hearted child.
You lived life **fearlessly**, dreamed **freely**, laughed **loudly**, and loved **fully**.

What happened?

Let me guess...
You started to grow up.
And with growing up came responsibilities.
Challenges. Expectations.
You were told to "be realistic."
You started hearing the voices that said:
"You're too much."
"You should be more like them."
"Don't fail."
"Don't fall."
And slowly... something changed.

You began to **hide parts of yourself**.
You felt ashamed of the mistakes you made.
You worried what others thought of you.
You stopped feeling **safe** being fully **you**.

Then what happened?

You finished school.
You thought you were ready for the real world.
But instead... more confusion, more setbacks, more pain.

Life seemed "fine" on the outside—
But relationships got harder.
Let's be honest:
It's easy to fall in love with someone...
But much harder to **grow** with someone.
To **understand**, to **stay**, to **be seen** and **still be safe**.

Maybe now you've got a job.
Or maybe you're running a business.
But tell me truthfully—

Do you sometimes feel like you're **running IN your business**,
Instead of **building ON your business**?

Do you remember all those big dreams you once had?
The things that lit your heart on fire?
The visions that made your eyes sparkle?

Did you let them go?
Not because you didn't care—
But because other things felt more "important" at the time:
Working. Earning. Parenting.
Trying to keep everyone else happy.
Not because you're a people pleaser...
But because you honestly didn't know what else to do.

And now... life seems **okay**.
It seems **fine**.
But something feels... **missing**.

Let me guess—
Is it **PURPOSE**?
Is it **PASSION**?

Because somewhere along the way,
You stopped dreaming like that little kid you used to be.
You stopped **believing** in the impossible.

Why am I telling you this?
Because… that was ME.

And maybe… just maybe… that's YOU too?

(If we were having this conversation face to face, I'd look into your eyes and ask for your real answer. But since I'm writing to you in this book, I'll keep **guessing** what happened to your soul.)

If you've read any of my earlier books, you probably already know bits and pieces of my story.
But this time? I'm going **deeper**.
This time, you're going to hear the **hidden stories**—
The ones I haven't shared before.
The real behind-the-scenes of my entrepreneurial journey—
The **ups and downs**, the **highs and heartbreaks**, the **victories and voices I had to silence.**

But it's not just about storytelling.
It's about **you**.

I want to take you on a journey filled with **truth** and **tools**:
- Real stories (yes, vulnerable and raw)
- Practical steps you can take right away
- Secrets I've discovered that helped me go from stuck… to **soaring**

And not just for small goals or half-lived dreams.

No—
This is for your **BIG DREAMS**.
The ones you buried.
The ones you were too scared to say out loud.
The ones you secretly hope are still possible.

By the end of this chapter, my prayer is that you'll feel:

- **ENERGY** in your bones
- **MOTIVATION** in your mind
- **POWER** in your spirit

Enough to help you start dreaming again.
Writing again.
Believing again.

Because you deserve to rise.
And the world deserves to see **the real you**.

You ready?

Let's begin.

—Kristy Guo
The One Who Never Stopped Believing in You

Chapter One: They Laughed. I Dreamed. I Built.

From Mockery to Mentorship
—How I Turned Every "NO" Into a New Beginning

They Laughed. I Dreamed. Now, I Mentor the Leaders of Tomorrow.

I wasn't born into wealth, power, or connections. I was born into **poverty**, into **violence**, into **a world where dreams seemed dangerous**.

There were no mentors.
No helping hands.
Just chaos... and the quiet voice inside that whispered, *"What if there's more?"*

They laughed when I dreamed.

- 25 years ago, I said I'd travel the world.
  They laughed.
  5-10 years later—15 countries, 30 cities.
  Business class flights. 5-star hotels.

  Today, still travelling, and now it is for my own business.

- 20 years ago, I said I'd build an international sales team.
  They laughed.
  1-5 years later—**millions in revenue**, and the foundation for **billions more**.

- 17 years ago, I said I'd move to Australia with a baby in my arms.
  They laughed.
  I landed a job, started from scratch, and built again;

  Not only did I survive, but also did I thrive.

- 10 years ago, I said I'd write a book.
  They laughed.
  Today, I've published **5 bestsellers** and created 14 best-selling authors and I believe another 100 are on the way.

- They laughed when I said I'd speak on global stages, build a worldwide network, or coach the next generation of leaders...

But I didn't listen to THEM.

I *believed.*
I *acted.*
I *moved forward*—one leap of faith at a time.

Then came the vision…

I knew what it felt like to suffer alone.
To lack mentors.
To face the world without guidance, and to feel like *no one sees you.*

So I built what I never had.

Signature Global Network—a home for **visionary CEOs, mentors, coaches,** and **rising leaders** ready to create legacies.

We built it so *no one would be left behind.*

Today, like all humans, I am not perfect, but I am on my mission to help people:

☑ Become **paid global speakers**
☑ Become the international best-selling authors & global influencer

☑ Publish their **own bestselling book**
☑ Launch **7–9 figure coaching businesses**
☑ Re-finding purpose and passion in life and careers

☑ Get featured in universities, retreats, podcasts, and global conferences
☑ Build unstoppable influence and lasting income
☑ And turn their story into their legacy

And now, it's your turn.

If you've ever felt **called to lead**, to teach, to coach, to **build wealth with purpose…**

Then this is your invitation to **step into the circle.**

Where Millionaire Mentors Rise, Legacy Leaders Emerge, and Empires of Wealth Begin. Become who you were always meant to be.

Let them laugh.

You?
You build.

Would you believe that **everything** I ever wrote on my list came true?

This is just the beginning.
I didn't have mentors then. But I became the person I wished I could find.
And now, I'm sharing this with you—because maybe, you've been looking for a sign too.

The next part of this story is the **turning point**, the **breakthrough**, and the **secrets** to dreaming big and making it real. & Hey, it is NOT a fairytale, it is a journey full of setbacks, problems, challenges, disappointments, betrayals, distrust, breaking promise, mental stress, anxiety, doubts and fear.
But here is the KEY, if I could CONQUER them to keep dreaming BIG, **you can too.**

Don't worry about what **THEY** say about you.
Don't live a life based on **THEIR** expectations.
Don't shrink yourself because of **THEIR** opinions or standards—especially when they don't want you to win.
Don't say sorry or feel guilty when you succeed but **THEY** aren't happy for you.

Let me ask you something:
Are you making choices simply because you're afraid of being judged by **THEM**?
Who are **THEY** anyway?
Are **THEY** really that important to you?
Do **THEY** truly care about you—from the heart, not just on the surface?

Look around.
Who are you surrounded by right now?
Do they lift you up?
Do they challenge you to grow and become better?
Or…
Are they just people who say **GREAT THINGS** about you but never tell you the truth?
Are they just so-called **BEST FRIENDS**—but in reality, they SUPPORT you with **NOTHING**?

Let me share a real story with you.

I have a CEO client who's been in the logistics networking industry for decades.
If you ask him how many people he knows from networking events, he'd say—too many to count.
But when I asked him, "How many of them do you *actually* work with?"
He paused… and could only name a few.

During one of our 1-on-1 coaching sessions, we talked about the importance of attracting the **RIGHT** audience and clients. In logistics, your overseas agents are also your clients and your partners. So we did a little exercise together:

I asked him to name his **top 5 overseas agent partners**—not just familiar names, but actual **TOP CLIENTS**.

At first, he smiled with confidence and started listing people in his head. But then I asked him:

"Are you sure? Just because you know them well or have been friends for years, does that really mean they're your biggest supporters? They might be your most *familiar* ones—but not necessarily the *REAL* or *TARGET* ones."

He paused.
He nodded.
And he started to realize something.

Something he'd overlooked.
Something he had been doing for years—believing he was spending time with the RIGHT people, but maybe… he wasn't.

Then I shared my own story.

"I've been in this industry for over two decades," I said.
"And I've trusted the WRONG people more times than I can count. I burned out. I gave my whole heart to clients who drained my energy—and yet, they made up less than 20% of my income. I gave them EVERYTHING I could… but somehow, it was never enough."

He kept nodding and said, "That's exactly right. Same here."
I continued, "I've learned this truth the hard way: if I try to serve EVERYONE, I will end up serving NO ONE."

That session changed something for him—and reminded me of how far I've come.

The reason I'm sharing these stories with you is this:
Whether it's in **LIFE** or **BUSINESS**, the **WHO** is far more important than the **HOW**.

When you surround yourself with the RIGHT people—everything changes.

I was trapped by this for soooo many years.

One Bible verse helped me so much: **TREAT OTHERS THE WAY YOU WANT TO BE TREATED**.

If my friends win, I will cheer for them with all my heart. But I want them to cheer for me too.
If they're not happy for me, if they feel jealous instead of joyful, then they're not **REAL** friends.
And honestly—what's the point of being sad to lose people like that?

You might say:
"But Kristy... they're my family. They've been my friends for a long time. They've been with me through my journey. How can I just LEAVE them?"

Here's what I say:
You don't need to LEAVE them.
But you *do* need to spend **LESS TIME** with them... and **MORE TIME** with the people and things that matter.

I'm not asking you to become a **COLD-HEARTED** person.
I'm not saying stop being kind.
What I'm saying is—understand this:

We are ALL victims of the past.

Many of the people around us have been shaped by pain, by fear, and by the limitations passed down from their generation.

But here's the good news:
We have a choice.

We can choose different paths.
We can choose who we want to become.
We can choose WHO we allow to influence us and HOW we let them shape us.

Let's be real—we can't change our past.
We can't change where we came from.
But we can TOTALLY choose who we want to become.

So the real question is...

Are you surrounded by the RIGHT people?

So the Lesson #1: Surround Yourself with the RIGHT People

The Builders Are the Ones Who Win

Here's what I want you to take from this story.

If people **laugh at your dreams**, GOOD.
If they **mock your vision**, even better.

Because when they laugh, and you build—**you win**.

Let me say this clearly:

- You don't need a big name to build a big future.
- You don't need fancy friends to walk in your truth.
- You don't need a perfect past to create a powerful legacy.

What you need is **faith in your vision**, **courage to act**, and the **right people around you**.

🌟 Here's what I've learned:

1. The WHO matters more than the HOW.
If your circle doesn't challenge, stretch, and support you—they're not your circle. They're your **cage**.

2. Time is precious. Spend it with builders, not doubters.
You don't have to cut people off. But you do need to **elevate your environment**.

3. Not everyone will clap when you win. That's okay.
You don't need their applause to build your empire.
Build it anyway.

4. Your MISSION is bigger than THEIR opinion.
Don't trade your calling for their comfort.

5. Don't be afraid to outgrow people.
If they were meant to grow with you, they would.

📊 VISUAL of my story: "From Laughed At… to Leading"

Dream	What They Said	What I Did	Outcome
Travel the world	"You? Never."	Believed. Worked. Packed my bags.	15+ countries, 30 cities, business class dreams
Build an international sales team	"Impossible!"	Learned. Led. Built again and again.	Millions in revenue, a team across the globe

Dream	What They Said	What I Did	Outcome
Move to Australia with a baby in arms	"That's crazy."	Trusted the call. Took the leap.	New life, new roots, new success
Write a bestselling book	"You're not an author."	Wrote anyway. Again. And again.	5 bestsellers, 14 bestselling authors mentored
Speak on global stages, lead visionary leaders	"You're dreaming too big."	Spoke truth. Showed up. Kept going.	Signature Global Network built. Leaders rising.

✏ The Lesson?
LET THEM LAUGH.
YOU? YOU BUILD.

👣 And now… it's YOUR turn.

If you've ever felt the world doubted you…
If you've ever been surrounded by people who didn't get it…
If you've ever been told "that's impossible"…

BUILD anyway.

Let them laugh.
Let them doubt.
Let them whisper.

But **YOU? YOU RISE.**

You build the business.
You write the book.
You speak the truth.
You become the leader they never saw coming.

And when you do…
you won't just win for you—
you'll make room for the next generation too.

Chapter Two: Two Paths, One Choice

*Fit In and Fade **or** Rise and Influence.*

Let me walk you through something very real.
We all walk one of two life paths. And sometimes, we don't even realize we're on one until we pause and reflect.

The FIRST Path—THE DEFAULT PATH:
- You are born into a family. (You don't get to choose.)
- You grow up influenced by how your family thinks, what they believe, and the people around them.
- You start becoming like them—your parents, siblings, friends, teachers, classmates, even characters on TV.
- Everyone around you may be STRUGGLING in life, but at least you have each other. You talk, you laugh… for a moment, it feels better.
- But deep inside, you don't feel truly FREE.
- One day, you try something NEW. You want to CHANGE. You dream bigger.
- Then THEY start saying:
  "Why change?"
  "You're doing fine!"
  "Don't be weird."
  "Just be like us."
- So, you DOUBT yourself. You think: maybe they're right. Maybe YOU are the WEIRD one.
- You try to FIT IN again. You give up on your dreams.
- But here's the TRUTH: THEY are still stuck.

They are where they are FOR A REASON—but you don't know what that reason is.

Now, you face a BIG CHOICE:
Do you keep FITTING IN and stay the same…
OR
Do you DARE to be DIFFERENT—even if they call you CRAZY?

Let's be clear:
THEY are not really happy.
They just don't want you to grow, because if you grow, they'll feel left behind.

The SECOND Path—THE INTENTIONAL PATH:

Yes, you're still born into the same family.

Yes, you still love them.
BUT...

→ You learn to UNDERSTAND them, without AGREEING with everything.
→ You respect WHERE THEY ARE, but you don't have to STAY there.
→ You stop trying to FIT IN. You don't carry THEIR burdens.
→ You build your own energy, your own peace, your own success.
→ You choose to GROW, one day at a time.
→ One day, THEY look at you differently.

They begin to RESPECT you.
They FOLLOW you.
You become a POSITIVE INFLUENCE.

You become the person THEY were secretly hoping to become.

Here's the thing:

Most people compromise and stay on the FIRST PATH.
They FIT IN. They DISAPPEAR. They lose themselves—just to keep others comfortable.

But you... you can choose the SECOND PATH.
It's not EASY.
But it's that SIMPLE.

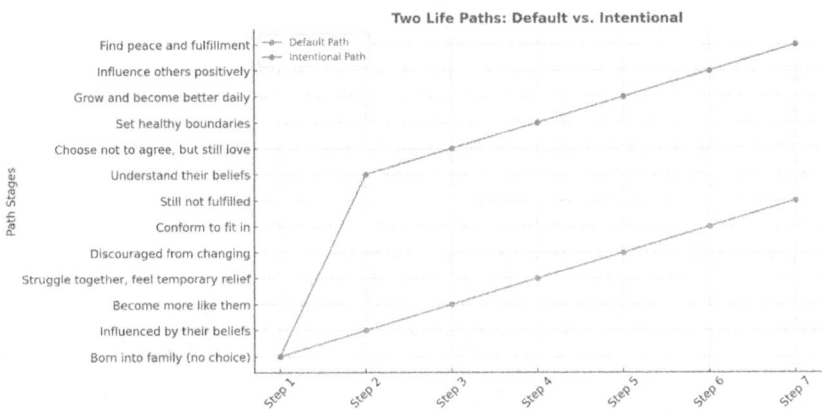

Desire – Dare To Dream, Rise & Shine

Visual Summary (Chart):

You can refer to the demonstration chart above to visually compare the stages of the Default Path vs. the Intentional Path. It clearly shows the red path (Default) as a stagnant loop of struggle and conformity, while the green path (Intentional) leads to growth, clarity, and positive influence

So Here Are Two Paths You Can Choose

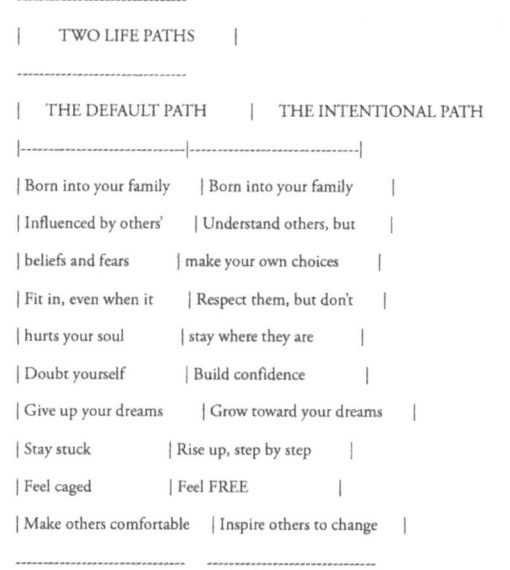

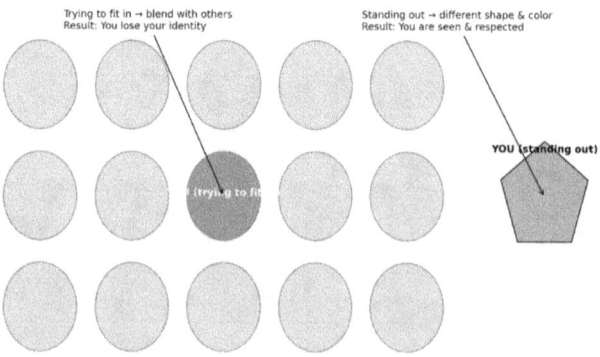

Why Trying to Fit In Will Make You Disappear

Here's a simple visual explanation of why trying to **fit in** makes you **disappear**:

- The red circle blends into the crowd—it's there, but no one notices.
- The green star stands out—different shape, different energy, **seen and respected**.

This demonstrates:
"Fitting in will make you disappear, but standing out will help you influence."

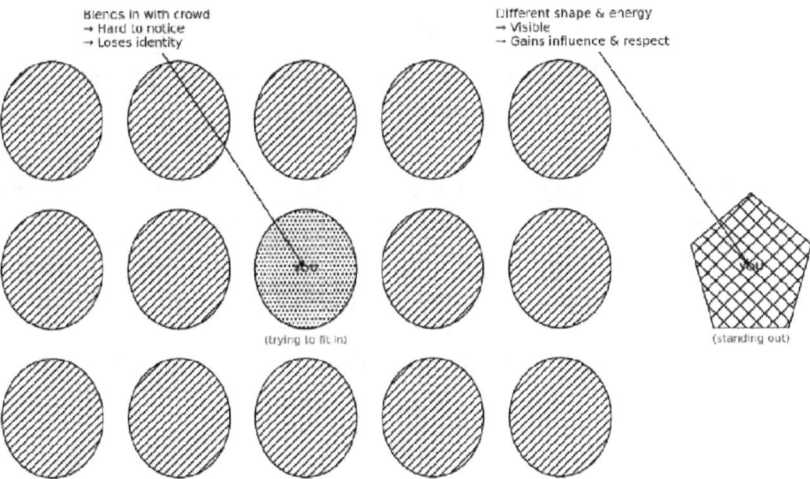

One line I'll leave you with:

Lesson #2

"FITTING IN will make you DISAPPEAR. STANDING OUT will make you SHINE."

The Day I Said NO—and Found My Voice, Power, and Freedom

Why Learning to Say NO Was the Key to Finding My VOICE, POWER, and FREEDOM.

Chapter Three: The Death of "Sweet Kristy"

Review. Reflect. Reset. Reclaim.

You might ask me:
"Kristy, it's easy for you to say than to do. Do you really do that yourself?"

And I say:
"YES. I'm not just talking about it. I LIVED it."

Let me tell you a short story. **My story.** So it will all make more sense.

I was always the **SWEET version** of me. **Kind, caring, people-pleasing.**
But like many of you, I carry **childhood wounds**.
So does my sister.

My sister was **raised by our grandparents**. She missed out on the **love and presence of our parents**—no matter how much they cared. That **emptiness** can't be easily filled.

I, on the other hand, **grew up with our parents**, but strangely… I felt more **pain than peace**.
I had to deal with **emotions and chaos** that were **far too much** for my little heart.
I was **scared, quiet, shy.**
I **lost my sense of identity**.
I **lost my voice**.

So I became **"Sweet Kristy."**
Always **smiling**. Always **saying YES**. Always **afraid to hurt or disappoint others**.
I wore that **"SWEET"** label like a badge of honor.

But what I didn't know…
was that it was actually a **TRAP**.

That trap held me for **over 20 YEARS**.
I kept **saying yes to things I didn't want**.
I made **decisions based on what OTHERS thought**.
I was **living under their eyes**, not my own truth.
And I was **MISERABLE**.

Until one day, **something shifted inside me.**

I started an **EXPERIMENT**.
I began to **say NO to things that didn't feel right**.

And guess what?
The people closest to me were **shocked**.
Some were even **angry**.

But I learned something **powerful**:

"If someone truly LOVES you, they want what's BEST for you. Just as you do for them."

About **eight years ago**, I **moved to Australia** for work.
Even though I had traveled to over **15 countries**, I was still deeply influenced by **Eastern culture** and surrounded by the **same types of people**.

But in **Australia**, starting from **ZERO**, I saw things **differently**.
The learning curve was **steep—and sometimes painful—**but it **changed me**.

I started to look at life through a **new lens**.
There is no one **"right" culture**.

But the moment I started **saying NO—with love and truth—**
my whole **LIFE changed**.

❦ What I Discovered

I wish I had learned this earlier.
The earlier I honored my HEART and my TRUTH,
the earlier I would have found my FREEDOM.
I would have attracted more like-minded souls.

I didn't forget my OLD friends or family. I still support them in every way I can.
But I stopped spending long hours with people who just complain or judge.
That energy drains me.
I've got dreams to build, and lives to impact.

I remember in one of my jobs, a group of ladies would gather daily to gossip for hours.
That was never me. I was too busy building a LIFE I loved.
Why judge others when you don't know what battles they're fighting?

❦ The New Me

Fast forward to today:

Desire – Dare To Dream, *Rise & Shine*

I now work with high-performing CEOs and legacy builders around the world. I've invested in myself—reading books, taking courses, learning from the BEST.

From:

- Jim Rohn – mindset & purpose
- Simon Sinek – leadership
- Grant Cardone – sales & marketing
- Myron Golden – Kingdom Business Mindsets
- Vin Giang – Communication
- David Pawson – Unlocking the bible
- Russel Brunson, Dan Lok, Alex Hormozi
  Plus another 20+ more… …
- Books like: *Bible (The best), Think and Grow Rich, Atomic Habits, The 4-Hour Workweek* and many more … …

These teachings lit a fire in me. And the RESULTS? **UNDENIABLE.**

I can't imagine still being the "**Old Sweet Me.**"
I'm no longer afraid to be **seen** or **heard**.

LOL **A Moment I'll Never Forget – The Death of "Sweet Kristy"**

One day, I was visiting my dear friend Ellen.
We talked about how some people still expect me to act like the OLD me.

I said loudly:

"They expect me to say YES—because they don't believe I'll say NO! It was hard! But I was no longer the OLD Kristy!"

And Ellen, with her cheeky grin, shouted:

"Which Kristy? She's DEAD!"

We both burst into laughter—tears forming in our eyes, and the laughter lasted for at least 10 minutes (Not exaggerated). That moment was silly, but the words were SO TRUE.

To grow, we must be willing to let the OLD VERSION of us DIE.
To say goodbye to habits, patterns, and masks that no longer serve us.

Review. Reflect. Reset. Reclaim.

📊 VISUAL DEMONSTRATION: "The Evolution of Kristy"

Version of Me	Core Belief	Result
Sweet Kristy	"Say YES to please others."	Lost identity, burnout
Awakening Kristy	"Start saying NO to protect peace."	Conflict, confusion, clarity grows
Authentic Kristy	"Say YES to what's TRUE. NO to what's not."	FREEDOM. POWER. JOY.

We must be willing to disappoint others if it means NOT disappointing ourselves.

Letting go of the "SWEET" me was the greatest gift I ever gave myself.
And the moment I did?
The people who truly SEE me, FOUND me.

If that sounds like you,
You're not alone anymore.
You're in the right room.

Why is this so significant?

Because the #1 thing that's BLOCKING you from dreaming big…
is your IDENTITY.

Let me explain.

Long ago, before mirrors were invented, people had no way to see themselves. So they looked to water, or to others, for reflection.

And that's exactly what we still do today.

We look for others to tell us who we are. Their opinions become our mirror. Their words shape our worth.

Can you remember when you were little, full of big dreams?
Maybe you said you wanted to fly a plane, write a book, or change the world…

And someone—maybe a teacher, a friend, or even your parent—laughed?

THAT was the moment.
The moment you started to shrink.

We are BORN as dreamers—sharp, full of energy—like the hedgehog with all its little spines.

But over time, to make others happy, we begin to dull our edges.
We try to be soft, smooth, quiet—like a mouse.

We lose our thorns... and we lose our courage.

And honestly?
It's SAD.
But it happens to almost everyone.

As Jim Rohn wisely said:

"It's not what happens to you. It's what you do about it."
"Disappointments don't only happen to the poor—it rains on the rich too."

In my book *The Joyful Leader In You*, I shared stories of my own suffering. But what I emphasized again and again was this:

"It's not about what happened TO you, but how you RESPOND."

That's one of the most important lessons I teach—
and I remind my daughters of it often.

Let's pause for a moment. Ask yourself:

- Are you a PEOPLE PLEASER?
- Do you feel GUILTY saying NO?
- Are you surrounded by people who aren't growing in the areas you care most about—like FINANCE, FAITH, or FAMILY?
- Are you AFRAID to let go of the OLD version of you?
- Do you worry your OLD FRIENDS or loved ones will leave if you CHANGE?
- Do you say things that aren't truly "you," just to avoid losing someone's love or trust?
- Have you STOPPED DREAMING BIG because of past rejection?

If any of those sound familiar...

It's time to REVIEW.
REFLECT.
And RESET your MIND and PRINCIPLES.

So here's my invitation to you:

Review. Reflect. Reset.

Look at the version of yourself you've been holding onto—especially the one who keeps shrinking, pleasing, pretending.

Then ask:
"Is this the version of me that's aligned with the life I truly want?"

If not—it's time to RELEASE that old identity.

And REPLACE it with someone braver. Someone truer.

You don't need permission.

You just need **a moment of truth...**
and the courage to say:

"That version of me? She's DEAD. And I'm just getting started."

So Lesson #3

In a life of distractions, doubts and judgement, always-> Review. Reflect. Reset. Reclaim.

Chapter Four: From Poverty and Pain to Purpose and Power

A Journey of Courage, Awakening, and Hope

Fast-Forward Before: The Girl Who Chose to Rise

Age 1–3: Pure Joy

The happiest years of my life—no pain, no pressure, just chubby cheeks and innocent laughter.
I was a joyful little angel, smiling with both eyes closed in every photo.
I believed the world was safe. I believed my parents were my heroes.

Age 4–11: Poverty, Pain & a Deep Longing for Mentorship

My dad worked as a factory security guard. My mum worked in the same factory. No matter how hard they tried, some nights we couldn't even afford enough food.

My father became frustrated, empty, and angry with life. He turned to alcohol and nightclubs. Violence soon filled our home. I grew silent and depressed.

My sister—only a year older—was raised by our grandparents, living a life that appeared "princess-like." But to me, it deepened my wound:
Why was I given the leftovers?
Why was I treated like I was less?
Why did she get new clothes, while I wore second-hand ones?

I began to internalize the belief that I was unworthy, undeserving of love. I longed for someone—**anyone**—to guide me, someone I could turn to with all the burning questions about life.
I didn't even know the word "mentor" existed.
But I knew I needed one.
And I couldn't find any.

Age 11–13: Confusion, Depression, and Silent Battles

This was the darkest time.
I lost confidence, my self-esteem shattered.
I even had thoughts of ending my life.

My parents' marriage was a constant roller coaster—divorces, reconciliations, endless fights. Sometimes I felt like the glue that held them together.

But I also secretly wished they would just separate—so the chaos would end.

In school, I had no one to guide me through this storm. I was expected to choose a path, a future, a career—**alone.**
No mentors.
No answers.
Only courage.
And that courage forced me to take ownership of every decision I made.

I cried often. People mocked me: *"She always cries."*
But no one saw the storms I was weathering inside.

The pain was so overwhelming that one day, I whispered to myself:
"If I don't change where I am, I will die."
So I started to dream.

Age 14–17: My Rebirth
Moving to a school away from my hometown felt like a rebirth.
I was still poor. I couldn't afford new clothes while classmates flaunted the latest fashion.
But something inside me began to glow.
I started to serve. I started to show up.

My parents' situation didn't change much, but now I could *breathe.*
I learned to let go of what I couldn't control, and focus on the one thing I could:

Myself.

And then... two teachers came into my life.
They *believed* in me.
They *trusted* me.
They gave me strength I didn't know I had.

I began helping others find their light, their peace. I told myself:
"If I can't find the light, I'll BE the light—for myself and for others."

That was the moment everything changed.
When my **attitude** shifted, my **life** transformed.

Age 17–18: My First Breakthrough
I got my first job. My first income.
And I began to dream even **bigger.**

I stepped onto the TV stage while working.
But every time I wanted to do something bold, a small voice whispered:
"Are you sure? Who do you think you are?"

It took everything in me to silence that voice.
But I won.
Every single time.
My secret?
"If I never try, I'll never know."

That mantra gave me courage.

Later, I started collecting **quotes**—they became my **invisible mentors**.
I didn't care who said them.
If they spoke to my soul, I wrote them down.
I read them every day.
I lived by them.

Here are some that changed my life:
- **"Prepare for the worst, but wish for the best."**
  It helped me manage expectations and stay positive through setbacks.
- **"Tomorrow will always be better."**
  This gave me hope when I was exhausted and on the edge of giving up.
- **"Nothing is impossible. Where there's a will, there's a way."**
  This gave me fire. When I set my goals, I *knew* I'd achieve them—sometimes sooner, sometimes later, but *always*.
- **"Never give up."**
  What it gave me: Hope. Resilience. Drive.

  Whenever life cornered me, when things felt too heavy to carry—I'd return to these three words.
  Simple. Short. But deeply powerful.

  "As long as I don't give up, the game is never over.
  And if the game isn't over… I haven't lost."

  That truth helped me push through seasons when failure felt final.
  It reminded me: **Persistence is a power move.**
- **"Life is like a mirror. When you smile at it, it smiles back. When you frown, it frowns back."**
  What it taught me: Personal energy is powerful. What I give, I get.

  This quote anchored me during moments of disappointment—especially when people were rude, unfair, or cold.
  Instead of reacting with resentment, I reminded myself:

  "My energy shapes my experience.

If I stay grounded, positive, and kind—even in chaos—life eventually reflects that back."

Yes, life gets messy.
But the way I choose to show up—**with grace, not grudges**—determines the harvest I reap.
I still believe this today:
The seeds you sow will become the fruit you live with. Choose wisely.

📊 VISUAL LIFE JOURNEY CHART: "My Awakening"

Age Range	Season	Key Emotions / Experiences	Life Lesson
1–3	**Pure Joy**	Innocence, laughter, trust	Joy is our natural state. We are born whole.
4–11	**Poverty & Pain**	Emotional wounds, hunger, rejection, longing for a mentor	Struggle can plant the seeds of self-worth.
11–13	**Silent Battles**	Depression, confusion, fear, suicidal thoughts	Courage begins with taking one small step.
14–17	**Rebirth Through Service**	Support from teachers, purpose rising	When you can't find the light—BE the light.
17–18	**First Breakthroughs**	Work, first income, inner doubt vs outer action	You don't need to be ready. Just begin anyway.

Life Lessons from the Girl Who Chose to Rise

Looking back...
I didn't have the answers.
I didn't have a roadmap.
I didn't have mentors, money, or models to follow.

But I had something else.
A whisper inside that said: "There's more for you."

And maybe that whisper lives inside you too.

Here's what I've learned so far:

🦋 1. You don't need perfect conditions to grow.
Sometimes, pain is the very thing that wakes up your power.

🦋 2. Even when life feels unfair, you get to choose your response.
Don't let anyone else write your story. Not the past. Not the pain. Not even your parents.

🦋 3. If no one believes in you—start by believing in yourself.
Just a little.
Just enough to take one more step.

🦋 4. Your past is a chapter, not your conclusion.
What felt like the end... was just the beginning. It does not define you but your belief of yourself does. Focus on now for the future.

🦋 5. If you can't find the light—BE the light.
It's not about being perfect. It's about showing up, again and again.

You don't have to be the smartest, the richest, or the loudest in the room.
You just have to **be real**.
Be you.
And keep choosing to RISE—even if your voice shakes.

Because that's how FREEDOM is born.

Life Lesson #4: RISE Anyway

So to conclude Life Lesson #4 of my journey, here it is:

You don't need to wait for perfect timing, perfect support, or perfect clarity.
All you need is a whisper of hope... and the courage to take one more step.
Even if your voice shakes, even if your hands tremble—
RISE anyway.
Because every time you rise, your story becomes someone else's light.
And THAT... is how the girl who had nothing, became the woman who gives everything.

Chapter Five: When Hustle Meets Heart

The Inner Journey From Tireless Hustler to Tender Mother

Age 17–26: WORK, WORK, and MORE WORK

My whole life was about one thing: **WORK, WORK, and WORK**.

Even when I had a 9-to-5 job, I never worked just 9 to 5. I gave my **MOST**, every single day. I worked at least 14 hours, sometimes even 16. If I was travelling, I gave it my **ALL**—morning till night.

Yes, life was BUSY. But it also helped distract me from the family chaos back in my hometown… and the inner pain I didn't know how to name.

Because I worked so hard and always had a GREAT attitude, the company promoted me every six months. I was chosen to travel with the CEO because of my strength and capability. I earned **respect**, **recognition**, even **power**. And at the end of every year, my bonus was BIG—at least back then, I thought it was HUGE!

I could walk in and out of the office on my own schedule. I didn't just "get things done"—I stayed ahead of the game. I made sure my boss knew exactly what I was doing, and what our team had achieved. He trusted me so much that he encouraged me to build and grow my own business development team.

I was in nearly every top management meeting. I gave my **HEART** to the company and my bosses. I was all in.

Then, something changed.

I met **Luke**—my Mr. Right, who is now my husband.

That was the first time I thought seriously about making time for *my* family and *my* future.

We got married when I was 23. But I still didn't want kids just yet. I wasn't ready—I still had so much I wanted to **give** to the company. I had become a **workaholic**, always standing by, always ready to do more, always chasing the next big opportunity.

There was a voice inside me whispering:
"If you ever lose your passion for work… you will lose everything—including your identity."

So I kept running.
City to city. Office to office.
Train the staff. Manage the team.
Have dinner with family. Then repeat.

Everything felt **expected**.
But little by little... the fire inside me started to fade.

I began to ask myself:

WHY am I working so hard?
WHO am I doing this for?

Age 27 – The Year My Heart Split in Two

When New Life Meets a New Identity

Becoming a Mother for the First Time

When my first daughter, **Sze Sze**, was born, my whole life changed.

At that time, I was working with **HLS Group in Shenzhen**. After I married Luke, who lived in Hong Kong, the company kindly supported my move to their Hong Kong office. That meant following Hong Kong's work policies instead of China's. And while maternity leave in China could be up to **4 months**, in Hong Kong back then, it was just **10 weeks**.

I was heavily pregnant, but I didn't want to go on maternity leave until the last possible moment—just **one week before my due date**. I was always this **small but fierce** woman. Even with a big belly, I never thought of myself as weak or different. I didn't allow pregnancy to slow me down—even though I couldn't sleep well, needed the bathroom all the time, and my body was clearly struggling.

The **first week off work** felt... strange. And honestly, a bit **depressing**. From the age of **17 to 27**, I had never really taken a break—no real holiday, no leave longer than three days. Work had become my life.

I forced myself to shift my focus. I started reading books, attending baby classes, and learning how to be a mum. The truth is, I didn't really know what a perfect mother looked like. Growing up, both **mum and dad figures were missing** in my life. So, I created this **imaginary version of myself**—someone I wished I had as a parent—and aimed to become her.

It helped, but it also **overwhelmed me**. I tried to do it all, on my own.

Then the due date passed. One week, then two. Still no sign of labour. So I walked up and down stairs every day to help things move along. But with every passing day, my maternity leave was slipping away—**precious time lost**.

The Day She Arrived

It was flu season. The hospital had strict rules—**no relatives allowed inside**. Luke's dad, my father-in-law, was the one who took me to the hospital when I saw a bit of blood. Luke worked far away, so he couldn't make it in time.

When we got there, a nurse looked at him and awkwardly asked, "Are you her husband?"
He laughed in his **typical Cantonese humour**:
"Don't be kidding la! I'm too YOUNG to be her husband. I'm her father-in-law!"

That made me smile. I was so grateful he was with me.

The water still hadn't broken, and I felt no pain. So they kept me overnight. I stayed in the hospital **alone**, all night. No one was allowed in. The next morning, they scheduled me for **induction of labour** to avoid any risk to the baby.

Hours passed. Eventually, around 1PM on **April 3rd, 2014**, I was in a room with 4–5 nurses and midwives. They could tell I wasn't local—my Cantonese wasn't native, and they treated me differently. **Roughly. Coldly.**

There I was, lying on the bed, in a place full of people but feeling **completely alone**. My body was there, but inside I was just **telling myself to BE STRONG**. I've always been good at hiding pain. I've been offended so many times in life that I developed a kind of emotional shield. But this time, it **cut deeper**—because I wasn't just a worker anymore.
I was a **mother** now. And I wanted to **protect my baby** before she was even born.

The nurses left the room at one point, and I was lying there, trying to call for help.
No one came.

I didn't scream. I didn't cry. I just saved my strength.

But by **5PM**, the pain hit its peak.
I told them, "I can't hold. This is so painful. Please help."
They were just about to inject me when someone noticed—they could **see the baby's head**.

Minutes later, **Sze Sze was born**.

And I thought I would burst into tears like the women in movies.
But I didn't. I was **too exhausted**.

The First Moments of Motherhood

It wasn't over. They **placed her in my arms** immediately and told me to breastfeed.
I was in shock. I didn't think I had milk. I didn't feel ready.
I just wanted a moment to breathe—but instead, I was given another **task**.

Eventually, after 30–60 minutes, they pushed me out with Sze Sze in my arms.
And that's when I saw **Luke**, running towards me.
And in that second… **I broke**, bursting into tears!

After holding in so much **pain, pressure, confusion, unequal treatment**…
After trying to be **brave and strong for everyone else**…
I finally allowed myself to be what I was—
A **vulnerable wife**,
A **new mum**,
And deep down, just a **little girl**
who never got that **father's hug** when she needed it most.

The reason why I shared these stories with you is BECAUSE, it is the tough experiences that taught me deeper meaning of life:

1. Even the strongest people break—and that's OK.
Strength isn't just about pushing through. It's also about **allowing yourself to feel**, to rest, to cry.

2. You can't do everything alone.
Even if you've always been the one to carry everything, **asking for help is not weakness**—it's wisdom.

3. Becoming a parent brings up your childhood.
When you step into the role of "mother" or "father," it brings back all the things you wish you had. That's your chance to **heal and rewrite the story**.

4. Love changes everything.
Career, pride, identity—all of it takes a new shape when love enters. Whether it's the love of a child or the love of a partner—it softens us and teaches us what truly matters.

Visual Chart: The Transformation of Identity (Age 17–27)

Age Range	Role/Stage	Focus	Key Emotion	Lesson Learned
17–26	Hustler, Workaholic	Career, Success	Drive, Distraction	Hard work = success, but at a cost
27 (Early)	Pregnant Woman	Transition, Preparation	Uncertainty, Pressure	It's okay not to know everything
27 (April)	New Mum	Baby, Survival, Healing	Pain, Love, Vulnerability	Vulnerability reveals strength

Looking back at those ten years of non-stop hustle…
I thought being strong meant always saying "yes,"
always doing more,
always pushing through without complaint.

But becoming a mother taught me something different.

True strength is not how much you can carry alone.
It's how gently you can hold yourself—
when everything inside you is breaking.

So to conclude Life Lesson #5, here it is:

Life Lesson #5: When Hustle Meets Heart

Hustle will build your name.
But heart? That will build your legacy.

You can be powerful *and* tender.
Driven *and* deeply human.
You don't need to prove anything anymore.
You just need to live—and love—with your whole heart.

And if one day you feel like you're not enough…
Remember:
You are already everything your inner child ever needed.
And now, you get to become her safe place.

—*Kristy, The One Who Chose to Rise*

📓 Journal Reflection Prompt (For High-Achieving Men & Male CEOs/Leaders)

💬 **Reflection Prompt:**

Think back to a season in your life when you were chasing success so hard…

you didn't stop to ask yourself how you really felt.

- What were you trying to achieve—and who were you trying to prove it to?
- What version of "success" were you chasing?
- What did you really need at that time—but didn't feel safe enough to ask for?

Now take a moment to write a letter to your past self…

Not as a boss.
Not as a provider.
Not as a warrior.

But as a father figure. A protector. A man who knows what truly matters.

Tell him:

"You don't have to carry all of this on your own anymore.
You're allowed to rest.
You're allowed to receive, not just give.
You're allowed to feel—and still lead."

📓 Journal Reflection Prompt (For High-Achieving Women & Female CEOs/Leaders)

💬 Reflection Prompt:

Think back to a chapter in your life when you were achieving, performing, leading…

but deep down, you felt like something was missing.

- What were you chasing—and who were you trying to become?
- Whose approval were you hoping to earn?
- What did you most *need* at that time—but were too busy, too proud, or too afraid to ask for?

Now write a letter to your **past self**…

Not as the boss.
Not as the strong one.
Not as the woman who "has it all together."

But as the **mother, sister, or wise woman** you needed back then.
The one who offers gentleness, grace, and truth without judgment.

Tell her:

"You don't have to prove your worth by how much you carry.
You're allowed to rest.
You're allowed to receive, not just give.
You are enough, even when you're not 'doing.'
You don't have to hold it all alone anymore."

Chapter Six: When Dreams Demand Everything

The Inner Journey From Starting Over to Standing Tall

Age 27–32: New Life in Australia

When I first landed in Melbourne, I wasn't just entering a new country—I was stepping into a whole new identity.

- I had fought hard for this move—exams, interviews, complicated procedures. It felt like a mission impossible, but I did it. I nailed every single step.
- My husband gave up his job to come with me. We left behind everything familiar—our home, our careers, even our little girl who cried every morning at childcare. I still remember the countless tears. It was painful.

But this was the price I was willing to pay for my dream life in **Melbourne**.

From the right hand of a CEO to a nameless clerk—
From leading boardrooms to doing operational admin—
From being known and respected to feeling invisible—
I killed all my egos. One by one.

The cultural shocks were real. The loneliness was loud. I second-guessed myself every day.
I wasn't just learning a new job.
I was re-learning how to *be*.
To speak carefully. To smile when I was hurting.
To blend in—even when everything inside me was screaming to stand out.

There were nights I couldn't sleep.
Mornings I didn't want to wake up.
I felt the depression creeping in quietly.
The girl who used to speak boldly suddenly became silent.
I wore a mask just to be accepted—
to stay safe,
to keep the job,
to keep the visa.

But even in that darkness, I made a promise to myself:
"Work harder. Contribute more. Whatever it takes."

I needed to prove that I could make a difference.
And I did.

My contract was extended.
Then extended again.
Then came the permanent residency.
Then, finally… citizenship.

The day of my online citizenship ceremony during COVID, we sang the national anthem.
And I just cried.
Not out of sadness—but because it had been such. a. journey.
That moment meant everything.

But the journey wasn't just professional.
It was deeply personal.
And humbling.

Did I mention I failed my driving test *six times*?
Three times the writing. Three times the road test. One major accident.
It broke me. For one week, I couldn't even look at a car. I swore I'd never drive again.
But I did it afraid.
Because this dream life in Melbourne? It required me to show up—even shaking.
Even in fear.
Even when I felt like giving up.

I thought rebuilding relationships would be easy.
It wasn't.
I thought my voice would naturally be heard.
It wasn't.

There were moments I saw injustice—at work, in life. But I said nothing.
I was scared to lose what I had worked so hard for.
So I silenced myself.
And in that silence, I started to lose my identity.
Confidence faded.
I became someone I barely recognised.

But deep down, one part of me never gave up.
The part that dreamed.
That believed.
That held on—no matter what.

Age 32–34: The Shift

Then… stability.
We got our IDs. Our PR status. Finally, a breath of relief.

But now that the survival mode was easing off…
The 9-to-5 job no longer fulfilled me.

Something inside me was whispering:
"There's more."

We had the courage to try for a second child.
I changed jobs. Got promoted into a leadership role that truly recognised my worth.
Then COVID hit.

And ironically… it became the *best* season of my life.
I finally had space to slow down, reflect, and hear my own voice again.
I wrote my first book.

Age 34–Now: The Rise

From that point on, it was all about **COURAGE**.
Not the kind you show in front of people—but the kind that shows up when **no one's clapping**.

- **COURAGE to start my own business**
- **COURAGE to chase dreams without asking for permission**
- **COURAGE to become a certified coach and speaker**
- **COURAGE to be different—and do different**
- **COURAGE to run not one, but two conferences a year**
- **COURAGE to invite others into co-authored books**

I recently concluded my reflection with this quote:
"The world isn't lacking dreamers or doers—it lacks risk-takers."

So many people have **dreams, ideas, and thoughts** every single day. But ONLY a few DARE to take the **RISK**—to have the **COURAGE** to go with it.

Not just to try, but to keep going **until they get it**.

When I started **Signature Global Network**, I had only AUD 20,000—a bonus from the last company I worked for.

I told myself:
"This is the money I will invest in my business. I'll either lose it or make it work."

And deep inside, I said:
"I would NEVER allow losing the money to happen—because I want my family to have a BETTER life."

The reality?

In between, I STRUGGLED. I didn't understand much about running a business. I was afraid to charge people. I was unsure about the structure.

BUT I WENT AHEAD ANYWAY.

Year One:

- Profit was OK.
- I learned A LOT.
- We brought **60 global CEOs** together for our first conference.
- But I was burned out—no holidays, late nights, constant guilt when traveling with family.

Even though my monthly salary was less than my last job, **the annual income and the impact kept me smiling.**

Year Two:

- Profit was **better than OK**.
- My team started to **form and stay**.
- Network **doubled**.
- But I hit the wall of **scaling and retention**.

We added services:

- **Staff hiring**
- **Marketing**
- **Learning app**

Every month, something NEW. Those who worked with me said they learned more than ever in their career. Why? Because **I dream, and I take action.**

Year Three:
- **AMAZING.**
- My team stayed.
- I outsourced more.
- My leadership paid off.

Each of them became a **breadwinner** for their families. Maybe I only pay 10 people, but behind each one is a family. That made me **HAPPY**.

I ran two global conferences. Some members were **unhappy** about the cost. Some were **delighted** and we welcomed many new amazing faces.

Yes, it brought pressure. But **COMFORT never appeared in my dictionary.**

After every event, I was **exhausted**. I didn't even rest properly. Because for me, **my REST is doing things I love.**

Let's be honest—There were moments of:
- **Depression**
- **Fear**
- **Anxiety**

But it's the **CHALLENGES** that helped me bounce up to where I am TODAY.

I fought the battle of:
- **Low sales**
- **Training staff while needing to sell**
- **Pressure so heavy I cried**

I dreamed of finding good **FARMERs** in my team so I could focus on being the **HUNTER**. As the saying goes: **Great businesses need both.**

But I didn't just do both—I **taught** my team how to do both. That's why it's always **WE and US**.

I'm grateful.

My coaching business **took off**. CEOs queued to work with me. I launched the **co-authoring journey**.

But throughout everything, I NEVER STOPPED doing two things:

1. **LEARNING**

I invested in **MYSELF**—books, courses, programs. Even fashion, my happy place, didn't take up more than learning.

I didn't just spend **money**, I spent **time**. Every. Single. Day.

Because if I don't feed myself with growth—
I feel like I'm starving.

I realized:
"The only way to grow wealth is to become more valuable."

2. PRACTICING, INVENTING & CREATING

Knowledge alone has NO power without ACTION.

I practiced what I learned. I ran experiments. They worked—because I had **faith and determination.**

I love solving problems. When I see chaos, I become the **detective and judge.**

I believe creating solutions to help others is an **honor.**

Creativity is my happy garden.

I can create all day—and now that's part of my business. Creating offers tailored to clients' needs.

I used to fear sales. Now I LOVE sending offers. Here's what I learned:

- **100% of people love buying.**
- **No offer = no opportunity.**
- **When you think FOR your client, not for yourself, magic happens.**

I made MANY mistakes. But one trait saved me:

I'm NOT AFRAID TO START OVER.

That includes:

- Admitting failed strategies
- Apologizing for mistakes
- Changing what didn't work

I am PROUD to start over again and again.

Yes, I sacrificed. I said **NO** to personal events, kids' parties, friends.

But I tried to always show up for my kids' games, awards, pickups. **Balance is not perfection—it's intention.**

Because I'm not just a businesswoman chasing dreams. I'm a **mother**, a **mentor**, and a **leader.**

It's not easy. But it's simple—when your principles are clear.

If there's ONE TRUTH I've learned:

You can't rise with ego.

You rise by choosing:

- **Responsibility**
- **Sacrifice**
- **Grit**

The only way to turn down the noise…
is to **SUCCEED**.

The Egos I Had to Kill

- "I'm too senior for this."
- "I shouldn't have to start over."
- "I've already proven myself enough."
- "I want applause before the work is done."
- "I'm scared to be real, to be seen."

I've embraced imperfections:

- Typos in my book
- Mistakes in business
- Wrong decisions I had to own publicly

But killing ego didn't make me smaller. It made me **stronger.**

I'm not sharing this to impress you. I'm sharing this to **remind you**:

If you're in a season of:

- Starting over
- Losing yourself
- Crying in silence

You're not alone. You're just **becoming.**

Life Lesson #6: When Dreams Demand Everything

Dreams will cost you:

- **Your comfort**
- **Your pride**
- **Sometimes your voice**

But keep going. Because the ones who stay—Are the ones who **RISE.**

With **heart**.
With **grace**.
And with a **voice that will never be taken away again.**

—Kristy, The One Who Started Over and Still Chose to Rise

Chart: "The Climb of Courage: Kristy's Journey"

Year	Major Milestones	Challenges	Wins
1	Launched SGN with AUD 20K	No business knowledge, fear of charging	60 CEOs, first global conference
2	Scaled network, launched services	Retention issues, time limits	Team formed, doubled network
3	Ran 2 conferences, team stability	Pressure, member expectations	Broader impact, expanded offers

Core Beliefs That Kept Me Going:

1. Never stop **LEARNING**
2. Always be **CREATING**
3. Be ready to **START OVER**
4. Kill the **EGO**
5. Lead with **HEART**

Chart: The Egos I Had to Kill (And What I Gained Instead)

⊘ The Ego I Had	🧠 What It Told Me	💡 What I Did	👉 What I Gained
"I'm too senior for this."	"This job is too small for you."	I started anyway, from the bottom.	🧘 Humility + New skills
"I shouldn't have to start over."	"You've done enough already!"	I accepted the challenge.	💪 Strength + Fresh start
"I've already proven myself."	"You don't need to try again."	I worked harder than ever.	✨ Respect + New achievements
"I need applause now."	"No one sees your effort, quit!"	I kept going—even in silence.	🔥 Inner power + Trust in myself
"Being vulnerable is weak."	"Don't show your real feelings."	I shared my truth anyway.	♡ Courage + Real connection

Sometimes, your *pride* can tell you:

"You're too good for this. You don't need to try again. Don't show your feelings."

But the truth is:

When you let go of pride, you grow stronger inside.
You become kinder, braver, and more powerful.
You don't need to be perfect—you just need to keep going.

🌀 Reflection Prompt

🤔 **Think:**

- What's something you're scared to try because you think "I should already be good at it"?
- What could happen if you tried anyway?

✏️ **Draw:**

- A picture of "Old Me" holding the heavy egos.
- And "New Me" after letting them go—feeling free, light, and strong.

🪶 Identity Transformation Chart

Age Range	Life Phase	External Reality	Internal Struggle	Emotional State	Growth & Outcome
27–32	New Life in Australia	Started over from scratch. From top executive to entry-level clerk.	Felt invisible. Silenced voice. Culture shock. Fear of failure.	Painful, lost, emotionally exhausted. Identity crisis.	Resilience built. Passed all exams. Contract extended. Permanent residency earned. Gained citizenship.

Age Range	Life Phase	External Reality	Internal Struggle	Emotional State	Growth & Outcome
		Driving failure x6. Major accident. Rebuilding from fear.	Lost confidence. "I'm not good enough." Wanted to give up.	Fear, embarrassment, deep self-doubt.	Showed up afraid. Earned driver's license. Became stronger.
		Parenting & partnership. Child in daycare. Husband quit job.	Guilt. Pressure to hold it all together.	Tearful goodbyes. Emotional toll of sacrifice.	Family stayed united. Gained deeper purpose. Melbourne became home.
		Workplace injustice. Silenced herself to stay safe.	Lost her voice. Suppressed truth.	Anxiety. Depression. Identity fading.	Learned survival. Planted seeds of future courage.
32–34	The Shift	Achieved stability. PR secured. Changed jobs. COVID pause.	Realised 9–5 no longer aligned with soul.	Restlessness. Whisper of new dreams.	Promotion. Leadership role. Wrote first book. Clarity returned.
34–Now	The Rise	Launched business. Became a coach, speaker, author, leader.	Faced fear of visibility. Questioned worth.	Brave, focused, visionary.	Courage became her compass. Built impact platforms. Created legacy.

Magical Words you should say *to yourself my friend:*

"I don't rise because it's easy.
I rise because I promised myself I would.
Even when it's hard. Even when I'm scared.
Even when no one sees.
I rise—because I'm becoming the version of me I was born to be."

Chapter Seven: The Uber Chronicles

How a Conversation Can Change a Life
You don't need a big platform. You just need a big heart.

I once heard a proverb in China:
"You will become a doctor when you are sick for a long time."

It is very true.
I went through huge **challenges and pain** in life—which helped me understand:

These situations didn't happen **TO ME**—
They happened **FOR ME**, and **FOR OTHERS**.

I became more like that "doctor"—
Someone who carries **superpowers to heal and empower** others who are now facing what I once faced.
And now?
I've become **so passionate and energetic** when it comes to **motivating, influencing, inspiring, and empowering people!**

🚘 **March 2025—I Changed Lives Through My Uber Rides!**

But the **top 3 stories**?
They HIT ME THE MOST.

I never thought I had that kind of superpower with Uber drivers—
Until it happened.

- One driver was in **LA**,
- Two were in **NYC**.

It all started with a **normal passenger conversation**.
I asked:

"What do you do besides driving Uber?"
(You know me—I LOVE asking about **dreams**.)

Because to me?
DREAMS are EVERYTHING.

It usually started like this:

Them: "I think I wanted to…"
Me: "Why not?"
Them: "Because of xxx (barriers)… and all the reasons why."

So I asked again:
"Do you believe you can do it?"
Them: "Maybe… I think so."
Me: "Why not?"

Then they'd list out more reasons.

That's when I'd **gently challenge their reasons**:
"If you want it SO BADLY—you should go and DO IT."

And then, I told them a story I often share:

"There's a true story in the book *Think and Grow Rich*.

A general led his soldiers to an enemy's land.
The only way to get there was by boat.
They were outnumbered 10 to 1. Food was running low.
Almost a mission impossible.

But when they landed? The general **BURNED THE BOATS**.

And he said:
'We either WIN or we DIE!'

You already know how the story ends."

(This is how I remember the story—the original version is similar.)

So back to our ride…
When I ask again, "Do you believe you can do it?"
They say:
"I think… maybe… I will try."

And I always respond:

"If you say that—you already fail.
Your subconscious mind is preparing for PLAN B…
And planning for NOT succeeding.

Do you know the word 'TRY' is often the word for failure?

If you're truly determined—say:
I WILL DO IT. I CAN DO IT."

The Result?

Two drivers were so inspired, they decided to **start their own business—STRAIGHT AWAY!**

🚗 **One** had failed **three times** trying to become a **police officer**.
After our ride? He was **determined again**.
And I KNOW HE WILL MAKE IT!

(If you're reading this—I am **SO EXCITED for you!!**)

One of them—the aspiring officer—looked at me and asked:

"Hey… I know this may sound weird… but can I have your number so I can text you when I get it?"

I paused. For a whole minute.
So much **JOY and FULFILLMENT** filled me.
A voice inside me whispered:
"Wow… THIS is powerful."

So I smiled and said:
"Yes, of course."
I handed him my name card.

What Filled My Soul the Most?

The **unexpected appreciation**:

🎖 "Thank you so much for sharing all of these.
This conversation **changed my life!**"

🎖 "I've never shared this with anyone…
I don't know why…
But you've **pumped me up.**
I CAN DO IT!!"

🎖 "This was the **BEST day of my life.**
Thank you so much!!"

YES—I'm now **waiting for their updates**.
And I KNOW…
Within the next 12 months,
I'll hear that they've **achieved their dreams!**

I am **so HAPPY and EXCITED.**
This **sense of achievement**?
It's better than almost **anything else.**

What Brings Me Joy?

❈ Seeing people **succeed**
❈ Lifting them **up**
❈ Making an **IMPACT**—even with **zero reward**

Because honestly?
The reward of them doing well is MORE THAN ENOUGH for me. 🎵

Why Am I Telling You This?

Because this…
This is my **SUPERPOWER.**

But here's the **secret:**

YOU have it too.

Yes—**YOU.**

✤ The power to change someone's day
✤ The power to lift someone up
✤ The power to remind someone who they really are

The lives of those 3 Uber drivers?
They'll never be the same again.

They'll be **BETTER**—not **BITTER.**

That's why I love what I do.

I wear many hats:

- 💼 **CEO.**
- 🌐 **Entrepreneur.**
- ✏️ **Mentor.**
- 🎤 **Speaker.**
- 👩‍👧 **Mum.**
- 💍 **Wife.**

- 👥 **Friend.**
- 🙏 **Volunteer.**
- 👫 **Believer.**

But I don't feel like I'm working a job.

I feel like I'm living a **MISSION**.

A mission to **make a difference**.
A mission to leave a **LEGACY**.

And **legacy**?

It's not just for famous people.
It's not just for billionaires.

Legacy is this:

- ✅ ONE *person* you lift up
- ✅ ONE *soul* you remind not to give up
- ✅ ONE *opportunity* you give
- ✅ ONE *stranger* you believe in

That's what I believe in.

That's what I live for.

5 Celebrities Whose Lives Changed Because of ONE Stranger:

Keanu Reeves

A kind stranger once helped him fix his broken motorcycle. That small act gave him the hope he needed during a dark time.

Madelyn Cline

Before Outer Banks, she met an actor who told her to "stop waiting and just go for it." That moment pushed her to chase her dream—and it worked.

Oprah Winfrey

When she was 17, a radio host let her audition just because he saw something special. That moment launched her entire career.

Steve Harvey

He was homeless and broke. A stranger gave him money to get to a comedy show—and that show changed his life.

Charlize Theron

A talent scout saw her crying at a bank and encouraged her to audition. That moment turned her pain into power.

You **don't need** a microphone to change the world.

You **don't need** millions of followers.

You **just need** one thing:

A BIG HEART.

Every conversation can be a gift.

Every moment, a chance to lift someone higher.

And every person… is carrying a dream inside them.

Be the one who says:

"WHY NOT?"

Be the one who says:

"I BELIEVE IN YOU."

That's how legacies are made.

One Uber ride, one conversation at a time.

📊 VISUAL CHART CONCEPT

"The Power of One Conversation"

1. 🚗 One Uber Ride

    ↓

2. 💬 One Question About a Dream

    ↓

3. ♡ One Moment of Truth ("I believe you can do it.")

    ↓

4. 💡 One Shift in Belief ("Maybe I can!")

    ↓

5. 🌈 One Action Taken

    ↓

6. 🏆 One Life Changed

    ↓

7. 🔄 Ripple Effect (Now *they* inspire someone else!)

SUMMARY:

- 💡 Every person has a dream inside. Some just need a little help to believe in it again.
- 💬 Words are powerful. A simple conversation can light up someone's life.
- 💞 Legacy is not big things. It's the small, kind things we do that leave the biggest impact.
- 🔥 Courage means burning the boat. If you really want something, don't keep backup plans for failure—GO ALL IN.
- 🎺 You already have a SUPERPOWER. It's your heart, your voice, and your ability to lift someone up.

If there's one lesson I've learned from these Uber rides, it's this:

Lesson # 7 Leave no regrets by leaving a legacy.

You don't leave a legacy by doing something big someday—

you leave a legacy the moment you choose to believe in someone today, and that someone can be somebody that will help somebody else to leave a legacy.

Because that is the ONLY way to continue the legacy and a legacy that truly lasts!

✥ REFLECTION PROMPT

Write in Your Journal or Think About This:

1. Who is one stranger that once changed YOUR life?
2. What dream have you been "thinking about" but not taking action on?
3. Are you saying "I'll try"... or are you ready to say "I WILL"?
4. Can you think of one person today who needs your encouragement?
5. What is your unique superpower? (It could be kindness, courage, listening, etc.)

💬 Write one sentence today that could help someone else believe in their dream.

Chapter Eight: Becoming Uncopiable

There is ONLY one you in the world, don't try to be others

I was never meant to simply run a business.
I was called to build a movement.

Not for fame.
Not for followers.
But for freedom—
For myself.
For my family.
For the leaders who had forgotten their fire.

I started with just $250 in Shenzhen, working for someone else.
From there, I didn't just build logistics business *for* the companies I worked with. I built strong global network connections everywhere, generating millions in business and creating thousands of global partnerships.

Today, that vision spans more than 80 countries in my own network—SGN.
A family of leaders and innovators who choose connection over competition.

Along the way, people called me the C-Suite Whisperer.
The Legacy Architect.
The Empire Igniter.

But more than any title, I became someone I truly respect.
Not because I lived a picture-perfect life—
But because I chose to live it on purpose.
With peace.
With power.
By staying value-cantered and motivated by the impact I can make in someone's life.

I love this saying for my mornings:

I no longer wake up because I have to; I wake up because I'm excited for my dreams—and for helping others achieve theirs.

My True Work

I help high-level leaders reclaim their energy, clarity, and destiny.
I guide them to build companies and legacies rooted in purpose.

To achieve real freedom—without losing their soul.
To lead with vision and peace.
To create empires that last.
To become who they were always meant to be.

Everything in this world grows to its fullest—except humans. Why? Because God gave us free will.
My mission is to help every person reach their fullest potential and live their fullest life.
Because that is the only way to find the deeper purpose and true joy within you.

The Roles I Embrace

I've worn many hats—not for applause, but for impact:

- CEO Energy and Clarity Catalyst—for founders and freight CEOs ready to scale without burnout.
- Founder of Signature Global Network—the trusted logistics family in 80+ countries and growing to cover every country of the world.
- Creator of Signature Growth Academy—helping everyday leaders become published authors, visible speakers, and legacy voices.
- Five-time bestselling author—from *The Joyful Leader* and *Logistics Legends* to *The World's Thought Leaders*, building movements through words.
- Visionary behind Kristy Guo Enterprise—a multi-division platform spanning style, coaching, publishing, events, and media. Confidante to Global C-Suites—offering a safe space to those who lead the world but often feel unseen. – Coming soon!

Vision behind KG Brand:

- *ZERA* (coming soon)—a movement for Gen Z, Alpha, and future creators rooted in truth, faith, and creativity.
- *KG Styling* (coming soon)—helping women CEOs claim their identity, power, and personal brand with authenticity.
- Publisher at *KG Legacy House*—giving voice to global thought leaders through books, education, and licensing.
- Producer at *KG Media* and The Filter—crafting values-based content, podcasts, and storytelling that matter.
- Curator of *KG Global Events*—designing high-trust, high-impact summits and retreats for elite leadership.

More exciting journeys are waiting ahead.

More Than Titles

But beyond all that?
I'm still the woman teaching children at church.
The mother cheering at school events.
The soul who writes in silence, sings in worship, and seeks God's guidance in every decision.

I don't glorify ego.
I don't chase hustle for its own sake.
Because I don't need to.

I choose to build with faith, service, and legacy in mind.
I don't just help leaders grow their business.
I help them come home to themselves.

A Calling, Not a Distraction

People often ask how I manage so many ventures.
Yes, I'm multi-gifted.
But I never saw creativity as chaos.
I saw it as calling.
I was born to:

- Write stories and bestselling books (and I'm in the process of writing and publishing songs).
- Speak truth with both boldness and compassion.
- Solve complex problems with simple, clear systems.
- Build spaces for the next generation to dream boldly.
- Shape identities that crown the soul, not just the brand.

My clients often say:

"Kristy, you see what others can't. You hear what I won't say."

And that's the work I'm proud to do.

I see the CEO lying awake at night, buried in operations, wondering if the dream has died.
The founder exhausted from trying to look successful on LinkedIn while feeling lost inside.
The leader who's achieved wealth but is asking, "Is this all there is?"
The visionary desperate to leave a legacy but not sure how, or with whom, to build it.

I see them—and I whisper:

You're not here to copy anyone.
You're here to become someone no one else can replicate.
Let's rise. Let's build. Let's make you uncopiable.

What I've Learned

After more than two decades in leadership—surrounded by real entrepreneurs, CEOs, dreamers, visionaries, millionaires, even billionaires—I see one thing clearly:

We all share the same human weaknesses.
Dignity and integrity matter far more than money.
A wealthy mindset is more important than short-term profit.

Poor people spend money.
Rich people invest in people with money.

Time is never "just money."
Time is *far* more precious than money.

If I asked you:

"I'll give you a billion dollars today—but you must die today and give up the rest of your life."

The answer is obvious.
You can always earn more money.
But earning more time? That's much harder.

It's not about *living* a life.
It's about *how* you live your life.

When I see my eldest daughter already 11 years old, time becomes even more critical.

If you're ready to lead with purpose, to create something lasting, to leave a true legacy—let's begin.

This isn't just about scaling your business.
It's about expanding your impact.
It's about designing your life on purpose.
And helping you become the leader only *you* can be.

Because you were never meant to be average.
You were meant to be **uncopiable**.

⚙ My Signature Frameworks (Not Just Acronyms—Activations)
I created these frameworks not to sound clever—
But to give high-level leaders a **map back to themselves**:

✳ C-Words—*The Pillars of Living Fully*
Conscious • Concentration • Connection • Courage • Communication • Care • Commitment • Consistency • Core

❀ D-Words—*The Process of Dream to Destiny*
Desire • Dream • Decision • Discipline • Determination • Dedication • Do • Done • Destiny

🏆 F-Words—*The Culture of Legendary Leadership*
Family • Faith • Fun • Friendship • Future • Fortune • Freedom

✉ Want early access to my book expanding these frameworks?
Email me at **cuilanguo@outlook.com** and join the **waitlist.**

💬 What I Know for Sure

The world is filled with **noise**.
But legacy? It's built in **silence**.

In the late nights.
In the messy starts.
In the decisions no one applauds.

You don't rise with ego.
You rise with **surrender**.
You rise by showing up, again and again—when no one's watching.

If You Want to Be Unforgettable...

Be Uncopiable.

There's only ONE YOU.
Everyone else is taken.

I'm not for everyone.
But I am for the **one who's ready to:**

- ✅ Heal soul wounds that sabotage success
- ✅ Build an empire that reflects **truth**
- ✅ Launch a brand that **magnetizes trust**
- ✅ Rise again—**stronger, clearer, and braver**

So, if you're standing at a crossroads…
Choose to rise.

Because you're not just building a business.
You're building a **legacy**.

And I'll be right here—
Whispering to your highest self until you believe:

- ✨ You were born to lead with joy.
- ✨ You were made to create with clarity.
- ✨ You are NOT too late to become legendary.

Let's not just build companies.
Let's build **eternity-shaping empires**.

—Kristy Guo
The One Who Started Over and Still Chose to Rise

📊 **Visual Chart:** *My Journey from Self to Soul Impact*

Phase	Challenge	Identity Gained	What I Built
Shenzhen	Scarcity, Fear, $250 Budget	Courageous Dreamer	Thousands of Global connections, millions of business growth
Startup	Burnout, Guilt, Solo Builder	High-Trust Leader	SGN, Core Team, 60 CEOs members
Expansion	Scaling Pain, Team Pressure	Legacy Mentor & Community Maker	Global Conferences, Coaching Brand Offers
Mastery	Ego-killing, Soul Alignment	The Uncopiable Visionary	Book Empire, Coaching Business, 2x Year Summits
Now	Multidimensional Leadership/Global Speaker	Soul-Aligned Empire Igniter	TEDx Stage to be/ Global Movements, Future Brand (ZERA, KG)

Ready to Build Your Legacy?

Is that you? If yes, I am passionate to support GOOD WILL, BIG DREAMS and VISIONS:

- ✔ Speak at your conference and podcast or have you to our podcast and conference
- ✔ Guide your executive team or movement or direct you to someone who's already done and succeeded to help you. Don't let ego hold you back. You don't have to do it alone!
- ✔ Co-create your bestselling book, personal brand, or empire system

But no matter we can meet or not, I am determined to keep building, serving and creating for the future. Just like my childhood experience, when I felt there's no light, I decided to be the light! This is my mission, to touch 1 more souls each time! To help the next logistics legend to live their life fully, to dream fully and to laugh and love fully!

Thanks to the social media and technology, I recently started a new YouTube channel focused on serving CEOs and global leaders, I shared my vulnerable stories and keep reminding visionaries to keep believing and not to lose identity or soul:

Soul-Aligned Scaling:
I help high-performing CEOs, entrepreneurs, and creatives reclaim their energy, eliminate burnout, and build purpose-driven legacies—without hustle or hype.

🌟 *Motivation • Business Systems • Faith-Driven Leadership • Creative Power*
🔖 *Speaking • Coaching • Storytelling • Legacy Activation*
📍 kristyguo.com

"Don't just scale. Become who you were born to be."

With love and respect!

Kristy Guo

Author BIO
Kristy Guo

Global Voice of Logistics Leadership, CEO Mentor, and Movement Builder

President & Founder, Signature Global Network | Creator of *The Logistics Legend* Series | Award-Winning Coach | Keynote Speaker | Multicultural Networking Expert

Kristy Guo (Cuilan Guo) is not just rewriting the rules of the logistics industry—she's redesigning the *entire game*. As the visionary force behind **Signature Global Network (SGN)**—one of the fastest-growing logistics communities spanning 80+ countries in under three years—Kristy empowers freight forwarders, supply chain innovators, and global CEOs to scale with purpose, systems, and soul.

With over 20 years of experience in the logistics industry in leadership roles and a track record of transforming **freight forwarding business into multi-millions in profit** across global operations, Kristy is recognized worldwide as a logistics icon and change-maker. From earning just $250 a month in Shenzhen to now mentoring elite leaders and speaking on world stages, her journey is a masterclass in resilience, reinvention, and radical results.

Her signature frameworks—like the **6 F-Words for Culture**, the **SGN Flywheel**, and **KG Coaching**—are turning business owners into visionaries, companies into communities, and operations into global movements.

Kristy is the curator and co-author of *The Logistics Legend* book series, which elevates untold founder stories into lasting global legacies. A passionate believer in authentic leadership, multicultural synergy, and faith-driven entrepreneurship, Kristy's mission is to guide the next generation of C-Suite leaders through both strategic growth and personal transformation.

Her storytelling—rooted in faith, family, and fearless execution—has resonated with leaders across five continents and ignited collaboration among logistics pioneers, tech disruptors, and purpose-led entrepreneurs.

Whether you're seeking a mentor to scale your company, a speaker who fuses heart with hard strategy, or a community where your business finally belongs—**Kristy is the connection you've been searching for.**

♀ Let's build something legendary together.
@ www.kristyguo.com
@ www.signaturegln.com
LinkedIn (Cuilan Guo): https://www.linkedin.com/in/cuilan-kristy-guo-1776b5182

Chapter 2

From Hustle to Legacy: Lessons in Leadership and Growth

Fabrizio "Pep" Alvear

Contents

Chapter One: **Roots and Resilience: An Immigrant's Journey of Survival, Sacrifice, and Strength**

1. *A Farewell That Sparked Reflection*
2. *The Price of Opportunity*
3. *Fire, Fear, and Finding Our Way*
4. *Brothers, Belts, and Becoming*
5. *Back to Ecuador: A Clash of Worlds*
6. *Return, Rebuilding, and a Promise to Never Be Poor Again*

Chapter Two: **From Bergenfield to Boardrooms**

1. *Growing Up Fast in the United Nations of Bergenfield*
2. *Hustle, Embarrassment, and Earning Respect*
3. *A Fork in the Road: From Community College to a Real-World Degree*
4. *Building, Selling, and Buying It Back*
5. *Legacy, Leadership, and Lessons for the Next Generation*

Chapter One: Roots and Resilience

An Immigrant's Journey of Survival, Sacrifice, and Strength

A Farewell That Sparked Reflection

I recently attended a "celebration of life" ceremony for one of my business partners, Socka Suppiah, in Chicago, Illinois. He passed away far too young at 57 due to an unexpected heart attack. Hundreds of people gathered to honor his memory and share stories. Many speakers delivered touching tributes about how he had changed their lives and dedicated his time to supporting underserved communities. Socka was a well-respected leader and entrepreneur who founded several successful companies and mentored countless individuals over the years. His son gave a heartfelt speech, sharing many cherished memories with the audience. He spoke of his father's wisdom and generosity—qualities that inspired me, as well as many others, to think bigger and never compromise one's values. An immigrant from India, Socka came to the United States to attend Iowa State University and pursue the American dream. His son closed the speech with one of his father's favorite quotes:

> *"It's not important what people think when you come in, but what they think when you leave." – Jurgen Klopp*

The Price of Opportunity

My story begins with immigrant parents who came to the United States seeking greater opportunities for their children. My father worked as a manager for the transportation administration in Ecuador when he was approached by an American working at the Ecuadorian embassy. This individual had gotten himself into serious legal trouble after a terrible accident and asked my father for a favor to help make the problem 'go away.' In return, he promised to provide visas for my father, my mother, and their four children to enter the United States. My parents struggled with the decision because it went against their values, but they also knew it might be their only way out of a country facing financial and political turmoil. In many South American countries, these kinds of "favors" often are the only opportunities to a better life outside the country. After many days of careful thought and conversations with my mother, my father ultimately agreed to do the "favor" in exchange for visas to the United States. Though arrangements like this weren't legal and carried the risk of future consequences, it was an opportunity my family couldn't pass up. Two of my father's brothers had recently immigrated to New York, and this was their chance to join them and begin a new life filled with possibility.

Fire, Fear, and Finding Our Way

After arriving in the United States, my family settled in Spanish Harlem, New York—a low-income and dangerous neighborhood near where my father's brothers had made their homes. The families supported one another, working multiple jobs to pay the bills and trying to adjust to a new life in a foreign land. A relative allowed my parents and their four children to stay with them in a small two-bedroom apartment, doing what they could to help them get on their feet. But within a few weeks, the landlord found out that eight people were living in an apartment that was leased for only four occupants. The landlord gave them a warning to reduce the number of occupants or face eviction. Left with no alternative, our relative had to ask my family to leave. Just like that, they were out on the streets, desperately looking for a place to stay. For the next few weeks, my family bounced between the apartments of various relatives until they were finally able to secure a tiny place of their own. But just a few months after moving in, tragedy struck—an arsonist who didn't want Hispanics in the building set fire to the apartment while everyone was asleep. Thankfully, my parents and siblings escaped unharmed, but the experience left them shaken and deeply traumatized.

After the fire, they continued moving from place to place throughout New York, working multiple jobs and living paycheck to paycheck just to survive. Eventually, my mother's cousin Floria, who lived in New Jersey, convinced them to relocate to a small suburban town called Bergenfield. It was a much safer community, with fewer immigrants and a more peaceful environment. It was there, in Bergenfield, that my family finally settled and started to build a life for ourselves.

Brothers, Belts, and Becoming

I was born in 1972 at Englewood Hospital, just a few miles from Bergenfield, New Jersey, two years after my brother Rafael was born in New York. We came from humble beginnings. Our parents worked minimum-wage jobs, often in factories or maintenance, just to make ends meet. They both held multiple jobs: my father cleaned banks at night, while my mother worked long hours in factories. My four older brothers, who were already teenagers or older, helped out whenever they could. After school, they'd often assist my dad with cleaning offices or banks once they closed for the day. When I started kindergarten, my brothers would walk me to school while our parents were working. There was a 20-year age gap between me and my oldest brother, so they naturally took on some responsibility for us younger ones. On my first day of kindergarten, my mom asked my older brother Victor to take a photo of me in front of my class so she could have a memory since she couldn't be present. As I stood outside, posing in front of the building, Victor playfully told me to put my middle finger in front of my face—and I did, not knowing what it meant. He snapped the picture, and to this day, we still laugh about that picture. My brothers would also pick me up after school and walk me home, continuing to look out for me as I began my early years.

There's an unbreakable bond of love and grit between my brothers and me. We try to get together as often as we can, and during family reunions or camping trips, they love sharing our wild childhood stories with my children. It's incredible to reflect on the resilience we all had. Despite the hardships, we rarely complained. Everyone simply did what needed to be done; failure wasn't an option; survival was the priority. My father, Victor Hugo Sr., was a good man who deeply loved his children, but he carried a heavy burden throughout much of his life. He often felt that he had sacrificed his dreams by leaving Ecuador. Back home, he had a respectable position with the transportation department, owned a house, and was well regarded in the community. He had even done modeling work for commercials and magazine ads. In his eyes, he had traded a life of dignity and stability for one of endless labor in a foreign country, working multiple menial jobs and living paycheck to paycheck. He was discouraged by the life he found in the U.S. and frustrated by the language barrier that made it difficult to communicate or advance. He didn't see much opportunity for himself here. What he didn't realize, though, was that his sacrifices were laying the foundation for his children—and future generations—to thrive.

At home and around family, my dad was a loving father, but in public, he often came across as an angry man—someone who could get into a physical fight over something as simple as a parking spot or a minor disagreement. I always felt like I was walking on eggshells, never sure if he was having a bad day or if he might start a fight right in front of me. And it wasn't just in my imagination—he had actually gotten into a fistfight at the local supermarket once. Our parents were very strict and had little patience for us misbehaving. If we stepped out of line, a whipping with a belt was almost guaranteed. Our apartment was filled with testosterone, and fistfights between my brothers were a regular occurrence. I remember one incident in kindergarten that stood out. Eduardo, my older brother who was in fifth grade at Washington Elementary, decided to sneak into my classroom during recess and steal money from my teacher's purse. When I got home that night, I overheard the chaos as my parents confronted him. He was going to be suspended for a week, forced to apologize, and had to return the money. That night, he also received a harsh belt whipping. I worried about what my friends would think when I returned to school the next day. Thankfully, the principal and teacher handled the situation discreetly, and not many people found out. Eduardo served his suspension, apologized, took his punishment, and we all moved on.

In 1978, we were one of the few Latino families in Bergenfield, and there were very few minority students at my school. I was the only child in my kindergarten class for whom English was a second language. Despite the earlier theft incident, I enjoyed kindergarten and went on to complete first and second grade before my parents dropped life-changing news on us. My dad had been unhappy for some time and convinced my mother that we should move back to Ecuador. He told her he had been offered a good job at John Deere through a friend and promised that life would be better for us there. The decision surprised the family, especially since it felt rushed. We all knew my father was frustrated in the U.S., unable to grow professionally due to his limited English skills. He believed he would have better job opportunities and a less stressful life back in Ecuador. My four older brothers who ranged in age from 15 to 29 all decided they would stay in the United States. My eldest brother, Fernando, who was recently married and 29, took responsibility for Eduardo and arranged for Eduardo to live with him in Horsham, Pennsylvania. Fernando had come to the U.S. at 15, learned English, finished high school, and earned a place at Rutgers University. Through grants, loans, and working at the university library, he supported himself and earned a master's degree in cell biology. He became a chemist working in a lab in Pennsylvania and was a driven, ambitious role model who I still turn to for advice today. Fernando eventually built a large biotech company and later sold his company to a publicly traded firm a few years ago.

Back to Ecuador: A Clash of Worlds

I was nine years old when my parents decided that my brother Rafael, who was eleven, and I would be moving to Ecuador—a third-world country—because they believed it was the best choice for us. Looking back, I feel it was one of the most selfish decisions they made, putting my brothers and me in a difficult position both physically and mentally. The impact of missing two years of school and being separated from our older siblings had long-lasting effects on me. Within weeks of the decision, I watched movers packing up our belongings for the big move. At the time, I didn't feel strongly one way or the other. I didn't understand that this change was permanent—I was simply too young to grasp what was happening. For a long time, I thought it was just a vacation and that we would soon be back with our older siblings.

From Hustle to Legacy: Lessons in Leadership and Growth

A few weeks later, we piled into an SUV driven by my older brother Victor Hugo Jr. and headed to JFK Airport for our flight to Ecuador. I vividly remember the chaos at check-in. Our bags were overweight, and the airline staff demanded a substantial fee. My father became upset and started arguing. The situation quickly escalated into a pushing match. Victor Jr. jumped in to defend him, and an all-out brawl nearly broke out. The police were called and almost arrested my father and brother. Eventually, everyone calmed down, we paid the hefty fees, and finally, we were on our way out of the country.

Once in Ecuador, we arrived at a decent-sized house that my father owned. He had always refused to sell this house because, in his mind, there was always a plan B to come back to Ecuador if he didn't get accustomed to the USA. I think now that holding onto that house always gave him an excuse to want to return. Life may have been different, and we might not have struggled financially as much if he had sold that house before first leaving Ecuador. My brother and I shared a large bedroom, and the house was an upgrade from our apartment in New Jersey. We had a large backyard where we could play catch with our baseball gloves. We met a lot of new relatives and had lots of fun.

My father came from a broken home. His father had two families and spent little time with my father and his siblings, who were mostly raised by their mother. Life was difficult; they often struggled just to put food on the table. In stark contrast, his stepsiblings lived a life of privilege and comfort. While my father grew up in hardship, they enjoyed a lavish lifestyle filled with opportunities he never had. It wasn't until after their father passed away that my dad reconnected with his stepfamily. While in Ecuador, we were occasionally welcomed into their world. On weekends, we'd visit upscale country clubs with expansive swimming pools or stay at luxurious beach houses along the coast, complete with private security. These experiences offered a glimpse into a life so different from the one my father had known. While the visits were brief, they highlighted the deep divide between two very different upbringings under one family name. We would see wild horses running along the beach, and once, we even watched our uncle hunt a deer, then gut and cook it right in front of us. We learned to drive three-wheel buggies through the sand, and there was no shortage of adventure or food.

During our time in Ecuador, money seemed to be less of a concern, and I don't recall hearing my parents argue about finances the way they did back in the United States. Despite the excitement and comfort we occasionally experienced, I quickly noticed some striking differences in our surroundings. We would often walk to an aunt's house, passing homeless encampments tucked into the hills along the way. Families lived in cardboard or makeshift wooden homes, and children wandered the streets naked or wearing very little clothing. It was a reality I had never seen before in the United States, and my brother and I would barrage our mother with questions. She explained that these were poor people and that in Ecuador, poverty was widespread. Later, I came to understand that Ecuador lacked a strong middle class—there were mainly the wealthy and the very poor. My mother would regularly donate our used clothes to families in need in our neighborhood. Even at a young age, I began to feel a deep empathy for those around me, especially the children living in such harsh conditions. I was surprised and saddened to witness how many people lived with so much discomfort, hunger, and uncertainty.

We spent a lot of time with cousins and extended family, but there weren't many relatives close to my brother's or my age, so we mostly had each other to play with. Eventually, we began playing with neighborhood kids, but they weren't interested in baseball, so we had to adapt and play games like hide-and-seek or soccer. Raphael and I were both athletic and held our own in soccer matches, but the other kids didn't like that we spoke to each other in English while playing. It felt natural for us to speak English with each other—it was simply easier and faster than trying to get our words out in Spanish. But the neighborhood kids didn't see it that way. Tensions quickly escalated, leading to fistfights and us being regularly called gringos. Playing outside wasn't much fun anymore, as it often ended in conflict. Eventually, my brother and I gave up and went back to throwing the baseball around—just the two of us and our gloves.

Return, Rebuilding, and a Promise to Never Be Poor Again

After a few months, we were invited to our first birthday party. Raphael and I were shy around other kids, especially strangers, and even more so when we had to speak Spanish. The other parents encouraged us to dance to Spanish music, but Raphael and I just looked at each other like they were crazy and quietly sat in the corner. After the cake and celebration, it was time to leave—but not before receiving birthday favors. Instead of the usual coloring books or stickers like we got in the United States, each of us was given a live baby chick. We were totally shocked and scared to hold them—their tiny nails felt sharp in our hands. We had no idea what was going on and were ready to question our mom as soon as we got in the car. My mother told us to smile, thank them, and take our chicks home. Once we were in the car, we burst out laughing as she explained that this was completely normal in Ecuador. We took the chicks home, named them, and cared for them like pets. They quickly became part of our daily lives, wandering around our yard. After a few months, the novelty wore off, and we paid less attention to them—going back to baseball instead. About a year later, while preparing for special guests, we heard strange noises coming from the kitchen. Raphael and I went to investigate and saw our mother snapping the neck of one of the chickens to prepare it for dinner. Disgusted, we ran back to our room and lost our appetite for the evening—while our guests raved about the meal.

About six months after we arrived in Ecuador, my parents began arguing frequently. My mom wanted to return to the U.S. to be with her other children, but my dad resisted. Raphael and I missed our siblings too and begged my mom to convince him. As the months passed and other kids started school, my parents continued to disagree about whether we should stay or leave. My mom refused to enroll us, hoping to change my dad's mind. The arguments grew more intense over the next year, especially after my mom threatened to leave with us. Nearly two years after our move, my father finally relented, allowing us to return to the United States and be reunited with our brothers.

My father still refused to sell the house and would rent it out, which never made sense to me because we needed money in the USA to build a life. The problem we faced now was that after the cost of the flight, there wasn't much money left to find a place to live. My eldest brother Fernando agreed to take my mother to live with him, his wife, and Eduardo in Pennsylvania. He also pulled some strings to get her a job in a lab he managed, doing hourly work to help send money to the rest of us in New Jersey. My father, Raphael, and I moved to Hackensack, New Jersey, into my brother Xavier's one-bedroom apartment. Xavier was 23, working as a security guard in a fancy high-rise apartment building. He also had a second job cleaning a large military tourist ship in town. He couldn't afford a car, so he biked everywhere, sometimes for miles each day. Hackensack at the time was mostly an immigrant and African American populated city.

My father walked us about two miles to school every day, and Raphael and I walked home together. I had skipped third grade in Ecuador, and my father and brother convinced the school that I had finished third grade in Ecuador, which wasn't true. They didn't want us to fall behind our age group, so I went right into the next grade. My brother was going into sixth grade after skipping fifth. I fell behind in class compared to the other kids who hadn't skipped a grade. I struggled that year but managed to pass. I remember the other kids would see my dad walking me to school and ask if he was my grandfather since my parents had me later in life. I'd tell them he was my dad, and they'd be shocked. On my dad's 50th birthday, I was so happy and shared with my classmates that my dad turned 50, and they spent the day teasing me that he was "half a century" old and old enough to be a grandpa. I laugh now—I'm 52 and don't feel like a grandpa yet.

Living in Xavier's one-bedroom, one-bathroom apartment was tough. It was small, and Raphael and I slept on blankets we spread on the floor at night. We didn't complain much because we got to see our brothers more often. We visited our mom and brothers in Pennsylvania at least once a month. One night, while sleeping in our makeshift blanket beds, Raphael screamed. When I looked over, there was a rat on his forehead. We turned on the lights, waking everyone in the apartment. My brother and father, who slept in the bedroom, tried to catch it as it ran into the kitchen—no luck. My dad told everyone to go back to sleep, but Raphael and I couldn't sleep thinking we were going to get bitten that night. The next day, my dad set a rodent trap by the refrigerator. In the middle of the night, we heard it snap. We caught the scoundrel. My dad flushed it down the toilet, and we went back to bed. We were still nervous though, and it took us a while to feel comfortable again thinking we would get bit.

Money was always tight. One night, after Xavier got paid, he placed his check in a dresser drawer and hours later he couldn't find it. We hadn't seen him put it in, but he swore he had. His stress was obvious—he needed it to pay rent. My father was working odd jobs, but between food and rent, things were rough. We searched everywhere and couldn't find it. I remember looking under the couches, in the hallways to see if he dropped it, all over the house but nothing. Hours after looking for the check, out of frustration, Xavier accused my dad of taking it. My father was insulted and denied it. I remember watching intensely and nervously as my brother sat at the kitchen table and my dad was washing dishes from dinner and they kept yelling at each other. Finally, my father snapped and threw a ceramic coffee mug. It hit Xavier in the shin, opening a large gash. Blood poured out as he screamed in pain. I ran for paper towels to help him stop the bleeding, but the blood just kept gushing out of his leg like a faucet. Now regretting everything, my dad rushed to help. We called for an ambulance, and they rushed him to the emergency room of Hackensack Hospital. After waiting for hours until 1 a.m., he came out with a cast and crutches and announced he had a broken leg. It took months to recover—and put even more pressure on us financially.

We got home after 1 a.m. I went back to search for that check and pulled the drawer all the way out—and found the check stuck to the bottom of the drawer above, wedged in. It was the first time I ever saw my father cry. He apologized repeatedly for what he had done to Xavier, and my heart was crushed. Xavier was also crying and apologizing for blaming him. Xavier blamed himself for continuing to accuse my father of stealing the check. That night was very stressful for me as a child, and I had never seen my dad cry before. Xavier and my dad forgave each other as we all cried together. From that day forward, no one ever spoke about what had happened. Many of my family will just hear about this story for the first time reading this chapter. Xavier and my father made us promise never to tell the rest of the family what really happened that night. They told the rest of the family that Xavier had had an accident and broke his leg. That night, I learned how desperation and poverty can lead to mistrust—even among loved ones—and to violence. I hated the fact that lack of money had pushed us to this point and vowed that I would work hard to make enough money and not feel this way again.

 At the end of fourth grade, my parents had saved enough money for all of us to move together into a two-bedroom apartment in Bergenfield. It finally felt like we were a full family again. My parents were back to sharing a home and bedroom. They bought two trundle beds with pullouts and fit them both into the second bedroom so all four of us brothers could sleep in one tight-fitting room. I was elated to have my own bed next to my brothers. I felt safe with them—a feeling I hadn't had in a long time. The constant stress and worry I'd carried seemed to go away in that cramped room. I was ecstatic about this new beginning.

Chapter Two: From Bergenfield to Boardrooms

Growing Up Fast in the United Nations of Bergenfield

My parents still worked two jobs and were barely home during the week, but weekends were our time together—unless they picked up overtime. The neighborhood was full of immigrant families from all walks of life. We called ourselves the "United Nations" because our friends were Chinese, Colombian, Indian, Cuban, Puerto Rican, African American, Jamaican, Dominican—you name it. We lived in rent-subsidized housing so it was affordable. Most of our parents were out working, so after school we'd play sports in the neighborhood and come home to eat the meals they had prepared in advance.

Getting top grades wasn't our priority. We didn't have anyone at home checking homework. For most of us, just passing our classes was the goal. The elementary school was a short walk from the complex, but the town baseball fields were a few miles away. I didn't mind biking to practice or games—baseball was my favorite sport.

At games, I'd notice my teammates' parents cheering in the stands while my family couldn't be there because of their work schedules. At first, it didn't bother me much, but when I made the all-star and travel teams, it stung to see everyone else with their families while I had no one.

My coaches noticed my maturity and leadership early on and made me team captain. That came naturally from growing up fast, getting tough love from my brothers, and learning to make my own sandwiches and meals when I was little. My coaches mentored me and genuinely cared. When it got dark, they'd load my bike into their cars and drop me closer to home. Those bike rides home in the dark as a fifth-grader weren't always fun, but they gave me time to reflect on what I wanted to achieve and how I could do better.

Hustle, Embarrassment, and Earning Respect

One of my best friends since fifth grade was Mike Sorrentino. His dad owned a construction business and was a hardworking, middle-class guy who always looked out for his son's friends. I spent most summers at Mike's house playing stickball, wiffleball, swimming, or going on road trips with his family. My parents didn't have extra money for takeout, but the Sorrentinos ordered food almost every day and always included me. I dreamed of one day owning my own business and treating my kids' friends to Bergenfield Pizza just like they did.

Mr. Sorrentino passed away unexpectedly in his fifties from a heart attack. I made sure to fly from California back to Bergenfield to pay my respects. Mike and I are still best friends to this day. He took over his dad's business and is doing great with a beautiful family of his own.

In middle school, I helped my parents by translating and looking up help-wanted ads for them. My mom learned English more quickly than my dad, who was more stubborn and set in his ways. She was always looking for clothing sales and cutting coupons. I remember sitting at the table helping her cut them or translating at the supermarket when the discount didn't show up on the receipt.

One of the most embarrassing moments for me was handing the blue card to the lunch lady in middle school. It was for kids who couldn't afford lunch. Friends would ask about it, and I'd have to explain. Some kids looked at me differently, but by then I had close friends who didn't care or would back me up if anyone mocked me. My brothers all went through the same thing. Looking back, I'm grateful for that program—it really helped relieve some financial pressure on our family.

My Colombian friend Stewart and I walked home from school every day. One week, we really wanted to see a show at the roller rink but didn't have the money—and we knew our parents didn't either. We passed the same Ford dealership daily and noticed the cars were covered in dirt. I suggested we go in and offer to wash them for $1 each using their hose and soap. Stewart thought I was crazy, but I walked right in and made my pitch.

The salesman was shocked but must have respected the hustle. He paid us out of his own pocket to wash 20 cars in three hours. He said it could only be a one-time thing so he wouldn't get in trouble with his boss, but he gave us more than enough for the tickets. I always waved at him after that when we walked by.

That was my first taste of working for money—and I was hooked. After that, I was always hustling: delivering newspapers, selling subscriptions door to door, even playing cards for cash at the laundromat with friends. That drive to improve my situation, to study people who had more and learn from them, was always there. It taught me resilience, hustle, and the belief that no one would ever outwork me.

A Fork in the Road: From Community College to a Real-World Degree

In high school, I was a below-average student and sometimes hung out with the wrong crowd. I was street smart because of how I grew up, but far from book smart. The high school counselor met with every senior to discuss career options. When it was my turn, I'll never forget what he told me:

"Based on your grades, you should just try to get a job and forget college. School isn't for you."

I walked out of that meeting feeling disillusioned and like a failure. How could someone in a leadership role say something like that to a kid, as if my future was already written?

Fortunately, I had thick skin. A few days later, the sting wore off.

After graduation, I lost my job as a dispatcher at AAA for being late too often. Sitting at home, I tried to figure out my next move. Like many of my friends, I enrolled in the local community college and started looking for part-time work. I knew the help-wanted ads well and found one for a mail sorter and warehouse worker in a nearby town.

I went for the interview along with a freshman from Seton Hall. After interviewing many candidates, it came down to the two of us. They chose him because he was at Seton Hall while I was at community college. I was disappointed, but I moved on.

A few weeks later, I got a call from the owner—the same guy who told me I didn't get the job. He asked if I was still interested. The Seton Hall kid hadn't worked out; he liked to party and was missing days. I showed up the next day, ready to learn.

My new employer was a mail logistics company called IPC. It had been founded by four young entrepreneurs who'd left a billion-dollar logistics firm to start their own venture. Two of them opened the New Jersey office where I worked; the other two were based in Maryland. I was excited to be part of something new, especially alongside successful salesmen in their mid-20s who were taking their book of business with them from their former employer.

From day one, boxes of mail poured into the warehouse for processing. I was on the floor with the two local owners, sorting mail and preparing it for international airline hauls. We worked long days and nights, doing whatever it took to get the job done.

As the business grew, it became clear the three of us couldn't handle the volume alone. They asked if I knew anyone looking for work. I brought in three of my best friends, and they made me the team lead, trusting me to train them.

One of the owners, Phil, started teaching me everything about the business and quickly took me under his wing. Phil was one of the best communicators I'd ever met—clear, concise, and patient. He spent time not only teaching me the job but getting to know me personally.

Within a few months, he gave me the keys to the warehouse and put me in charge of my own crew while he and his partner focused on sales and customer relations. Little by little, I learned more: how to answer phones and greet customers, how to handle billing, even making pickups in New York City.

Business was booming, and I was learning every aspect of it. I soaked it all in like a sponge, energized by the responsibility I was given. The hours were long, but the overtime pay was incredible. I even started helping my parents with their bills. I was working six or seven days a week and eventually stopped attending community college—I felt like I was getting a real-world degree in logistics from my mentor, Phil.

Building, Selling, and Buying It Back

After three years, I had a solid understanding of mail logistics and had received a masterclass in life from a successful entrepreneur. Phil came from a successful family and taught me not only about business and money but also about relationships and personal growth—things I'd never been exposed to growing up in Bergenfield.

He had a rare ability to motivate and inspire people. Thanks to him, I felt energized, capable, and ready to take on the world.

While working long hours, one of my coworkers invited me to a pool party in Lyndhurst at his girlfriend's house. It was a hot, humid day in New Jersey, and I needed a break. That turned out to be one of the best decisions of my life, because that afternoon I met my future wife, Kathy—his girlfriend's best friend. We hit it off quickly and had a lot in common. Her parents were also first-generation immigrants from Cuba and Spain. She was studying psychology at Rutgers University Newark and came from a put-together family. Kathy and I grew close quickly, and she understood me well.

After dating for over a year and a half, still learning and growing at IPC, Phil asked me to meet him in his office for an important meeting that would change my life's trajectory. Phil and his partners were planning to expand the business to the West Coast. They'd been recruiting a VP of Sales from their competition for a few years, and she had finally accepted. He asked if I would move to Los Angeles to run operations reporting to her. The offer was moving expenses and $35,000 a year.

He explained I'd get on-the-job training and build my knowledge and experience. I was honored that he would trust me to run the facility and told him I needed a few days to think about it. I'd never lived on my own before, but driving home after our meeting, I knew this was my chance to grow. I was 21 and needed to shake up my life.

I told my brother Eduardo about the offer and said I was seriously considering it. He told me I had nothing to lose. The next day, I sat down with Kathy and told her. She was shocked, and we both cried, but she knew my mind was set. We promised to do our best to make the long-distance relationship work and visit each other often.

That same evening, I told my parents about the offer and that I was going to accept. Both were very supportive, telling me it was my decision but that they would miss me very much. Within a few days, I had accepted and was planning my new life in Los Angeles.

One of IPC's partners had toured facilities in the LA area and secured a warehouse in an unincorporated part of the city called Gardena. He explained the tax benefits of that location, and I was soon tasked with setting up the new West Coast facility. That's when I met my new boss, Kelly.

When she first saw me, her expression said it all: *Who is this kid?* The partners had told her they were sending an experienced operations manager, so she was understandably surprised to meet someone barely out of high school. Kelly was about ten years older than me and brought a wealth of executive experience. She had also recruited three top-performing salespeople to join her.

I could tell immediately from the way her team and the owners spoke about her that she was loyal, hardworking, intelligent—and someone I could learn a lot from.

Business picked up quickly, and I was suddenly responsible for staffing the entire facility. That's when I realized the unique challenges of our location. Being close to Compton, we attracted many applicants from the area, and I had to carefully navigate the realities of local gang culture and community dynamics to build a reliable team.

After some early bumps, I managed to put together a solid crew of about 30 warehouse employees and partnered with a dependable staffing agency for temps when needed. The West Coast operation thrived, and I built a strong relationship with the new team.

Kelly became a mentor, supporting me through both successes and stumbles. She encouraged me to push through challenges, learn from my mistakes, and pivot fast. As my role grew, I began negotiating contracts with airlines and trucking vendors and built a strong professional network. I also paid close attention to the sales team, learning from their client interactions and facility tours. Their experience was invaluable.

At the same time, I was managing a long-distance relationship with Kathy. For two years, I took countless redeye flights from Los Angeles to Newark, flying back on early Monday mornings just to be in the office by 9 a.m. It was exhausting, and the strain nearly ended our relationship at one point. Distance causes doubt, and while we both tried to stay committed, we were also going out with friends on weekends and meeting new people in our own circles.

During one of our nightly calls, Kathy began questioning whether the long-distance arrangement was sustainable. She told me frankly that unless I could give her a clear date for moving back, she felt we needed to go our separate ways.

I took a few days to think about it and realized I couldn't let her go. I called her and told her I'd move back within three months.

When I gave Phil and Kelly notice, they were shocked. The expansion was going well—they hadn't expected me to want to leave. I explained that I had to prioritize my relationship, but promised to train my replacement. They accepted my decision, though reluctantly.

Soon after moving back to New Jersey, I took over as Senior Operations Manager at our facility, overseeing another operations manager and three supervisors. The company was thriving and continuing to grow. About a year later, the partners announced they were selling IPC to Global Mail, a larger competitor recently acquired by Deutsche Post. Suddenly, there was real uncertainty about my future and how IPC would fit into this new, bigger company. Global Mail had acquired IPC, Quick Mail, and Yellowstone International—three logistics companies all located within proximity of each other on the East Coast.

I asked Phil what it would mean for us. His answer was short: "*Just work hard. A decision will be made soon about which operation will become the main hub. Have confidence in your ability.*" It wasn't exactly comforting. With overlapping operations, consolidation was inevitable.

The sale was finalized, with each of the four IPC partners walking away with over $10 million. Some agreed to stay for a few years to support the transition. As part of the deal, I received a $50,000 bonus—and signed a strict non-compete and non-solicitation agreement. That bonus helped me buy my first home in a nearby town, which at least gave the transition some positive meaning.

An integration team was formed with executives from the three acquired companies. They toured each facility to assess operations, management, quality control, and SOPs. I led multiple tours at our IPC facility, doing everything I could to showcase the culture and systems we'd built.

About a month later, the announcement came: IPC's facility would become the primary East Coast hub. I was tasked with integrating the other operations into ours and was named GM of Operations for the new company.

It was a bittersweet promotion. While I was honored to lead the integration, it was difficult to visit the other facilities and sit down with local leaders to plan their closures. I had built relationships with many of these people over the years, and I knew this process meant many would be losing their jobs. Still, I had a responsibility to execute the plan.

I was proud that the employees who had been with me at IPC for over five years would keep their positions and continue to grow within the newly renamed **Deutsche Post Global Mail**. After a successful six-month integration process, we moved all four operations into a new 150,000-square-foot facility in East Rutherford, New Jersey. Most of the Quick Mail staff made the daily commute from Inwood, NY, while Yellowstone's employees had a shorter trip. Unfortunately, most of the Global Mail team from Virginia were laid off.

Not long after, DHL WorldMail was slated to be integrated into our facility as well. Their operation was in York, Pennsylvania, about three and a half hours away. I was asked to lead that integration too. It came with bigger challenges: none of the York employees would be retained. Naturally, I wasn't welcomed warmly during my weekly visits. Still, I did my best to communicate respectfully and transparently. Despite the difficult circumstances, I completed the transition successfully.

The entire process—across multiple companies and hundreds of employees—was one of the most demanding and defining chapters of my career. It taught me how to lead through uncertainty, make hard decisions, and remain steady in the face of change.

Joining the new company—headquartered in Frankfurt, Germany—meant adjusting to a very different corporate culture. Flexibility and customer focus, which had been core to IPC's identity, were no longer encouraged. As part of a massive postal administration, the new leadership prioritized uniformity, efficiency, and strict adherence to established processes.

At IPC, we thrived on innovation and entrepreneurship. We regularly customized solutions to keep clients happy, even if it meant thinking outside the box. But under Deutsche Post, we were told to "stay in our lane." Tailored approaches were seen as inefficient. The philosophy was clear: standardized services over creative problem-solving.

I remember one executive comparing the model to Mercedes-Benz: "It's an elite product. It sells itself. Anything outside the system disrupts the machine." This mindset also extended to the sales team. IPC had paid top commissions to high-performing reps, empowering them to control the customer relationship. Deutsche Post questioned why salespeople should be paid so much if the brand and service were supposed to sell themselves?

I was later sent to Frankfurt for training at their main postal facility. The scale of automation there was impressive. Every process was standardized, with employees following the same workflow step by step. There was no room for improvisation; any deviation risked creating backlogs across the entire system.

During that trip, I met with a team of engineers who would soon visit our New Jersey facility to study our process flows, labor efficiencies, and overall operational structure. The rigidity in Frankfurt was a stark contrast to what I was used to, but I recognized its value. Automation brought consistency and scalability—key elements for long-term growth.

That experience gave me a new perspective on balancing innovation with structure. While I still believed in customer-centric flexibility, I began to understand the power of systems designed to scale.

In the months after my trip, the engineers began arriving at our New Jersey facility to conduct time studies and create detailed process flow charts. The cultural differences quickly became apparent. Many of our long-time warehouse employees earned close to minimum wage, but they stayed because of the supportive culture we'd built. Now they had engineers with stopwatches standing over them as they sorted mail—an approach that understandably caused discomfort and tension.

As managers, we did our best to reassure the team it was only a short-term exercise. But the engineers lacked emotional intelligence or interpersonal skills to connect with the staff. They didn't try to build relationships or earn trust first, which created immediate conflict.

Beyond workflow assessments, the engineers questioned the value-added services we offered certain key clients. One example was a manual task where we pulled specific addresses for top-tier financial clients who needed documents sent via 1–2-day courier instead of standard international priority mail. This expedited delivery by 4–5 days and was critical for those clients. Though time-consuming, the margins on these accounts were well above industry average.

At IPC, this was how we operated. We prioritized client needs and weren't afraid to go the extra mile—as long as it was profitable. The founders were entrepreneurs who understood the value of a customer-first approach and knew exactly where that value could be monetized.

But after the engineers submitted their report to senior leadership, everything changed. The directive from the top was clear: eliminate non-standard processes and value-added services. Their reasoning was that scaling to a billion-dollar operation required consistency, automation, and simplicity—not customization.

From a corporate efficiency standpoint, they were probably right. But it also revealed something important: the larger and more rigid the organization became, the more opportunity it created for nimble, customer-focused entrepreneurs like me to step in where they no longer could.

Within the next year, I moved to Los Angeles and partnered with my former boss and mentor, Kelly, along with the three top sales reps we had worked with at IPC. Together, we started a new company: Express Postal Options. With encouragement—and investment capital—from Phil, Kelly and I mapped out a plan to launch a customer-focused logistics company built on trust, experience, and execution.

Our new "dream team" consisted of four accomplished female executives and me. I had developed strong working relationships with them while running IPC's Los Angeles branch, and we had built a foundation of trust and mutual respect.

The first year was one of the toughest of my life. Shortly after launching, Deutsche Post Global Mail filed a lawsuit against us, unhappy that we were now direct competitors on the West Coast. Their USA CEO at the time couldn't comprehend former employees leaving to start a rival business.

I quickly learned a valuable lesson in business: don't take legal battles personally. We believed in what we were building and knew we had the right team and vision to move forward. Still, the stress was intense. Most of our early profits went straight to legal fees.

At the same time, I was once again managing a long-distance relationship—this time with my now-wife. She stood by me through it all, emotionally and financially, helping cover expenses while I focused on fighting legal battles and building the business from the ground up.

To strengthen our operations team, I recruited my nephew Marcus and my brother-in-law Bernardo to move to Los Angeles and help us build out the operation. Their personal support was invaluable as we pushed through a difficult launch and laid the groundwork for what would become a successful, resilient business. It was the best $10-an-hour investment plus room and board I ever made.

They were both in their early twenties and loved the excitement of Los Angeles—weekends often felt like a fraternity house. After work, we'd pile into the company cargo van, a two-seater where someone always had to sit on a mail tub wedged between the seats to get home or go grocery shopping.

After an especially stressful week dealing with the lawsuit, I told Marcus and Bernardo we needed a break—a relaxing weekend away. On a whim, I picked Ensenada, Mexico, for a road trip. We packed the cargo van with our essentials and hit the road.

When we arrived, spring break was in full swing. Partygoers flooded the streets, with "Girls Gone Wild" camera crews filming the mayhem. My nephew looked at me and joked, "Uncle Pep, so much for a relaxing weekend," before bursting out laughing.

We spent the next two nights at a beachside motel that quickly ran out of water. We had to wait hours for a truck with giant water tanks to refill the supply. When it finally arrived, we knew we only had minutes to shower before the tanks emptied again.

The next night, after returning from a beach party at Papas and Beer, our room key wouldn't work. We called maintenance, and a worker showed up with a file to manually shave the key so it would turn in the lock. You couldn't make this stuff up. Meanwhile, the motel was a nonstop party zone with "Girls Gone Wild" filming outside all night. Sleep was impossible.

After a year of grinding through the lawsuit, Express Postal Options finally settled and was free to move forward. By then, we'd grown the business to $15 million in revenue. As part of the settlement, we agreed not to take any business from DHL Global Mail (formerly Deutsche Post Global Mail) for a year and paid a lump sum of several hundred thousand dollars.

Despite that setback, the business continued to thrive. After a year, Marcus and Bernardo returned to the East Coast to be closer to family. My wife relocated to Los Angeles, and together we began building our life and family there.

From 2003 to 2012, our team successfully grew Express Postal Options into one of the largest international mail service providers in the U.S.—and the largest in California. By 2011, we had developed a proprietary e-commerce platform and operating system to manage parcels into Canada, positioning ourselves ahead of the booming cross-border e-commerce market. While traditional mail volumes were declining, we anticipated the shift and capitalized on it.

Our success drew attention from Fortune 500 companies and foreign postal administrations. By 2011, we had reached $60 million in revenue and had been named to the INC 500 list of fastest-growing companies in the U.S. for five consecutive years. Unsolicited acquisition offers began arriving, sparking serious discussions about the company's future.

We faced a pivotal decision: continue growing independently, which would require significant investment in programming and IT talent to expand our e-commerce capabilities, or sell and let a larger company fund the next phase of growth. After lengthy—and sometimes heated—deliberations, we agreed to sell Express Postal Options for $20 million to RRD and Sons, one of our top customers and the world's largest printer.

RRD was expanding its logistics division, and we were a perfect fit for their portfolio. The partners and I agreed to stay on, incentivized to grow the division with the capital and resources promised.

Selling the company we had built from scratch to $60 million in revenue was bittersweet. But I was ready for the next chapter—working as an executive in a Fortune 500 company, eager to learn and grow further.

At RRD, I entered a more structured environment typical of a publicly traded company. We operated under shared services for IT, HR, Finance, and other areas—the most impactful of these being IT. I quickly discovered both the benefits and drawbacks of working within a large corporation.

On the positive side, I learned a great deal: how to build and manage budgets, oversee our own P&L, and present detailed one-, two-, and three-year business plans to executive leadership. I also met incredibly talented people who expanded my understanding of large-scale corporate operations. One of them, Chuck—the President of Logistics at the time—became a close mentor and remains a great friend to this day.

However, I also learned that the capital investments we'd been promised at the time of the acquisition weren't easy to secure. The internal IT team, managed through shared services, was slow and expensive. Strict compliance processes delayed development timelines, limiting our ability to roll out new tools or close larger accounts.

Meanwhile, marketing for our parcel division had to go through a centralized group focused primarily on RRD's core print business. Our growth initiatives were left largely unsupported.

Despite these limitations, we grew the business from $60 million to $160 million in revenue over eight years—without the marketing support or capital we truly needed to scale. We submitted countless business cases explaining why operational investments were critical. Our facilities were still relying on outdated, manual desktop workstations, making it difficult to sell confidently to enterprise clients. During facility tours, prospects would often question our ability to scale.

We identified a $3 million investment in automation as essential to unlocking our next phase of growth. Even RRD's top engineers agreed after reviewing our facility. Yet the funds were never released. After years of delays, we found ourselves in a holding pattern—growing but constrained.

In 2020, after eight years, RRD announced it would divest its logistics businesses—totaling $1.2 billion in annual revenue—to refocus on its core print services. Our division, International Mail and Parcel, was the second largest behind their $600 million trucking arm. Suddenly, we were meeting with various venture capital firms, exploring what might come next.

Then, an unexpected idea emerged—during a last-minute lunch meeting.

I was having a routine quarterly review with my friend and IT vendor, Socka, one of the co-founders of Sagazza, our outsourced IT partner for the past two years. As we discussed RRD's decision to sell, I casually mentioned we'd likely continue using his services no matter who bought the business.

That's when he stopped, looked at me, and said:

"Why don't we buy it?"

I laughed it off. "I'm not ready to invest most of my savings into buying a company," I replied.

But Socka was already five steps ahead. He began laying out how it could work—how he could raise the capital, structure the deal, and minimize the financial risk for Kelly and me. Over the course of that two-hour lunch, he walked me through the mechanics. The more I listened, the more it made sense.

He had the IT expertise, business acumen, and investor network, along with our trust. Kelly and I had operational and sales leadership, deep industry knowledge, and a vision for how we could grow. On the drive to my next meeting, I called Kelly and laid it all out. The conversation lit a fire in both of us. The same competitive spirit that had driven us to build Express Postal Options was back—and a new chapter was taking shape.

Within days of that lunch conversation, we were on a call with the new President of RRD Logistics, Brian, a colleague with whom we'd built a strong rapport. We pitched our vision and introduced Socka as the potential buyer. He listened carefully and responded with encouragement. If we could make the deal work, it seemed like a viable path forward.

Next, we were connected with RRD's Head of M&A. Their enthusiasm was more cautious. This wasn't a typical private equity deal—it was led by someone outside their traditional network. They were skeptical that Socka could raise the funds quickly and required a formal letter of backing from a bank before moving forward.

Unfazed, Socka delivered a signed letter from the bank the very next morning.

That was the turning point. RRD had already sold off all its other logistics divisions—we were the last piece. After a few months of negotiation, we closed the deal and bought the business back for less than we had originally sold it.

RRD had never truly understood our business. But we had maintained strong relationships with many of their executives and leadership teams, always delivering on our commitments. Most of those contacts had since moved on. With the logistics divisions divested and their debt reduced, RRD's stock began to climb. They needed to close the final transaction quickly—and they trusted us to take it over.

The deal came together because of timing, relationships, and trust.

Kelly and I had earned a reputation as high-integrity leaders within RRD. Those pushing to finalize the transaction wanted the business to thrive under leadership that understood it—and that's exactly what we brought.

Legacy, Leadership, and Lessons for the Next Generation

We rebranded the company as ePost Global, a tech-enabled parcel logistics provider. We invested over $5 million up front in automation and technology upgrades across our facilities, and we've continued investing annually to support scalable growth. We also invested in innovative new leaders to strengthen the team.

Today, just five years later, ePost Global is the largest U.S.-based, privately owned, direct-to-consumer international parcel company, with over $250 million in annual revenue.

At the heart of our success is our company culture and a team aligned around our core values:

- Represent the company with integrity
- Treat everyone with respect
- Strive for customer satisfaction in every encounter
- Collaborate and strengthen the team
- Celebrate successes and learn from mistakes
- Encourage innovative thinking
- Commit to operational excellence

The average employee at ePost has been with us for over 10 years. During our annual management meetings, I look around and realize most of us have worked together for over two decades. That kind of continuity doesn't happen by accident—it happens when you invest in people who believe in the mission and in each other.

People often say to me, "*You're lucky to have met people like Phil, Kelly, Socka, and Chuck.*" But it's not luck. It's about putting yourself in the right rooms with people who make you better—and taking advantage of those opportunities. Being in the right place at the right time helps, but it's hard, consistent work, truly listening, nurturing relationships, and creating value through trust, integrity, and idea-sharing that leads to bigger things. That's what builds success.

Relationships are everything—and the most important ones are those that challenge you to grow.

That's the message I pass on to my kids:

Invest in people who push you forward—and walk away from those who hold you back. I've ended business relationships and friendships, even with people I grew up with, because they were more focused on complaining than creating. People who don't want to grow will drain your energy and stall your progress.

Your spouse will be the most important decision of your life. Your business partners may be the next. Choose wisely. Make decisions with clarity and long-term vision.

My family came to this country under difficult circumstances. We struggled to live the American Dream and were often looked at differently because we didn't speak the language. I got my work ethic and empathy from my mom, who worked hard to support her boys and give us the chance to prosper through her tireless work and tough love when needed.

As Socka likes to say, quoting Jürgen Klopp:

> "It's not important what people think when you come in—but what they think when you leave."

That's what drives me. That's my responsibility: to make a meaningful difference in people's lives and leave a legacy that matters—not based on how I arrived, but by how I leave.

Author BIO
Fabrizio "Pep" Alvear

Fabrizio "Pep" Alvear is the Co-President and Managing Partner of ePost Global, a tech-enabled international shipping solutions provider specializing in cost-effective global delivery.

A first-generation American entrepreneur who built his career from humble beginnings, Pep has spent over two decades leading and transforming logistics businesses for profitable growth. He has served in senior leadership roles at DHL, where he championed operational efficiency, and he brings deep expertise in e-commerce logistics and complex cross-border supply chains.

In 2012, Pep co-founded Express Postal Options International, growing it into a $60 million enterprise before its sale to R.R. Donnelley. He then led the strategic buyback of that division in 2020, co-founding ePost Global and overseeing its acquisition of RRD's International Mail and Parcel Logistics Business. Under his leadership, ePost Global has expanded its global footprint and evolved into one of the largest U.S.-based providers of direct-to-consumer international parcel delivery.

Pep is passionate about helping companies achieve sustainable profitability, navigate mergers and acquisitions, and build resilient, values-driven teams. He offers mentorship for business owners seeking operational excellence and strategic growth, grounded in real-world experience and a commitment to leaving a meaningful legacy.

Email falvear@epostglobalshipping.com
LinkedIn: linkedin.com/in/fabrizio-alvear-a5b3241
Website www.epostglobalshipping.com

Chapter 3

From Scarcity to Significance

A Journey of Faith, Grit & Grace

Michelle Moreno

Chapter One: The Promise Beyond Poverty

Dreaming on Sacred Ground

Have you ever paused to realize…
That the place you're standing in right now—the business you run, the decisions you make, the influence you carry—was once just a dream?

Not too long ago, it was just a spark in your heart.
You're no longer in the same house you grew up in.
You're not surrounded by the same people from 15 years ago.
You don't think or lead the same way you did a decade ago.

Because you've grown.
Your vision stretched, your responsibilities expanded, and your faith deepened.

The road may have changed, but your inner fire—that desire to build something bigger than yourself—still burns.

Look around.
This was once your dream.
And now, you're living it—and leading others because of it.

The rags-to-riches story is often portrayed as a cliché in television dramas, usually wrapped in a plot of revenge or dramatic turnarounds. But in real life, these stories aren't driven by bitterness—they're born from vision. A vision rooted in purpose and guided by the will of the Creator.

But who is the Creator? And what role does He play in the journey of everyone? I can say this with conviction: knowing my Creator—not just knowing about Him but walking with Him—has been the anchor and compass that brought me to where I am today.

Who would've thought?

That a mother of two…
A founder of five thriving businesses…
A project director of a heart-driven foundation…
An award-winning financial advisor in the Philippines…
And now, an author…

Was once a little girl who went to bed hungry almost every night.
Who rummaged through neighborhood dumpsters just to find a usable bag, or a secondhand book she could still read.

A child who had nothing—except a stubborn dream and a silent faith that maybe, just maybe, her story wasn't meant to end in poverty.

This isn't fiction.
This is real.
This is my story.
And if it could happen to me, why not you?

The Night I Promised Myself More

It was a cold night in the province of the Philippines. Inside a cramped 20-square-meter house, five of us were settling in for the night. The door slammed open—a sound we had come to dread. My siblings and I braced ourselves, already knowing what came next.

Our father was home. Drunk again.

We watched in silence as he stumbled through the room, swaying from side to side, the stench of alcohol thick in the air. But it wasn't the alcohol we feared—it was what followed.

Terror gripped us when he opened the cabinet and reached for the axe he had hidden inside. He wanted to fight someone outside. Who, we didn't know. But we knew this rage. We had seen it before.

Our mother stood in front of him, sobbing, pleading with him not to go. Her arms outstretched like a shield, trying to block the door with her body. "Please, stop," she cried, over and over again. "Please."

My older siblings and I clung to each other in a corner, shaking—not from the cold, but from fear. We knew what alcohol did to him. And like most drunks, he couldn't be reasoned with.

That night, something inside me awakened. It was the first moment of true awareness I can remember—my earliest scenario seared into my memory like a burn that never fades.

And in that moment, a quiet question rose in my young heart:
Why does my life have to be like this?
Why is my father the way he is?

I didn't have answers that night. But what I did have was the beginning of a silent promise to myself—a promise that one day, this would not be the end of my story.

Surviving the Cracks of Home

My father worked as a construction laborer in a marble company, while my mother stayed at home to raise the four of us. We didn't have much, but we had enough to get by. That changed when the marble company closed down.

Just like that, our only stable source of income was gone. And instead of searching for another steady job, my father spiraled into vices—gambling, card games, and cockfighting. What was once a home built on quiet sacrifice and hard work began to crack under the weight of hopelessness.

With no paycheck to count on, our tiny sari-sari store became our lifeline. For those unfamiliar, a sari-sari store is like a mini convenience shop set up right outside a home, where goods bought in bulk are sold at retail. It's common in Filipino neighborhoods—a symbol of resilience and hustle. But no matter how many snacks or sachets we sold, the profit barely touched what we needed to survive.

Electricity bills. Water bills. Rent. Food for six mouths. School fees. Every single need felt like a mountain—and we were trying to climb them all with bare hands.

There were days when the power company finally cut us off. No light. No fan. No relief. But we couldn't afford to wait. Somehow, we figured out how to reconnect the line ourselves—just so we could have a few hours of light, a bit of comfort in the dark. There were also days when our tables stood empty, our stomachs growling, and the silence of an empty pot echoed louder than words. We couldn't afford the luxury of a Christmas feast, nor the warmth of a birthday celebration. Special occasions came and went like ordinary days—quiet, unmarked, and heavy with longing.

Then there was the rent. Our landlord's angry voice still echoes in my memory—shouting, threatening to kick us out, banging on our door with ultimatums we couldn't meet. Months of unpaid rent stacked like the unspoken fears we lived with daily.

As if that wasn't enough, my father had added yet another weight to carry—raising roosters for cockfights. A pastime that cost more than it ever gave. The little money we could've used for food or school was poured into feed, cages, and gambling losses.

We were surviving—but just barely. And every day I felt like walking a tightrope between hope and collapse.

We had to do.

I still remember how, as a child, I found small ways to earn what I could.

One of my first "business ventures" was using leftover paper pads to make handmade envelopes. I'd fold and paste them carefully, then sell them to my classmates for a few coins each. The profit was minimal, but to me, it was everything. A few pesos earned meant I could finally treat myself to a small snack—something sweet, something mine.

There was one afternoon I'll never forget. I had just come home from school.

The table was empty. My stomach was growling. That wasn't unusual—hunger was a familiar companion in our home. But that day, something in me stirred. I couldn't bear to sit and wait. I remembered a classmate who owed me money from our *paluwagan*—our little cooperative savings group among friends.

So, I went out and found him.

He paid me back, and with the money I received, I bought a small can of corned beef. It wasn't much—but it was enough. That simple meal became our lunch, something my mother and I could share.

To stretch our resources further, we walked to school every day. There was no transportation allowance, no shortcut. Just busy roads, scorching heat, and tired feet. I remember those walks vividly—tiny steps, heavy bags, and a silent determination pressing forward with each stride.

As I walked those roads, I talked to myself quietly. *Don't give up. Don't lose hope. You can't afford to lose hope—it's the only thing you have.* And truly, it was. Hope was the only thing I could hold on to when everything else felt like it was slipping away.

Looking back now, those walks were more than just a daily routine.

They were a metaphor for my life.

Every step toward school was a step toward my future.

With each stride, I wasn't just walking to class—I was walking toward something better. Toward a life beyond poverty. Toward a dream I couldn't name yet but believed in with everything I had.

Strangely, I never blamed my parents. I never considered rebellion. I knew deep down that making poor choices would only add more pain to an already difficult life. I didn't want to be another weight pulling us down.

I wanted to be the one that rose—and maybe, one day, lifted us all with me.

High school came, but little had changed at home.

By God's grace and my eldest sister's sacrifice, I was able to enroll in a private Christian school. She had just graduated and started working—and without hesitation, she used her earnings to fund my education.

This new environment stretched me. I learned to stand on my own, to find my voice, and to lead. I joined school organizations, became part of the lyre performers in our school drum and lyre band, danced with the cheering squad, and immersed myself in every opportunity that made me feel alive. These moments gave me a taste of who I could become—someone capable, confident, and driven.

It was also in high school where my second business venture began—and where, unknowingly, my love for sales and entrepreneurship took deeper root.

I partnered with a neighbor who sold soft, huggable pillows in all sorts of adorable shapes. With her trust and permission, I began promoting them at school—sharing them with classmates, and talking about them with genuine excitement. Eventually, I sold enough to fill an entire Philippine jeepney—two full sections' worth of orders!

For most, it may seem small. But for a teenage girl like me, it was everything.

It wasn't just about the money. It was about proving to myself that I could create something—move something—make something happen. It was the first time I felt what it meant to build, to sell, to grow. And in that moment, something ignited within me.

A spark that would one day become a flame.

A simple sale that would one day lead to a calling.

But while I was beginning to discover pieces of my potential outside, things inside our home remained difficult—even humiliating.

Debt had followed us for as long as I could remember. And now, it was knocking on our door—literally. Almost daily, someone would come, screaming at my mother, demanding payment. Sometimes they'd bang on our sari-sari store door, hurling insults that echoed through the neighborhood. My mother would simply bow her head and whisper, *"I'm sorry, we're trying."* There was no fight left in her—only fatigue and quiet desperation.

I remember one night in particular. I was sitting at our table, reviewing for a school exam, when loud, aggressive pounding on our door jolted me from my notes. My body froze. My heart raced. I knew that sound. It was the sound of shame coming for us again.

I don't remember what happened next—only the feeling. The sickening mix of fear, guilt, and helplessness. The kind of moment that imprints itself on your soul.

Each day, I walked through our neighborhood with eyes that avoided contact, shoulders heavy with unspoken shame. Many of our neighbors were angry at us—tired of waiting to be repaid. Even when we managed to settle some debts, it was never enough. We were caught in a vicious cycle of borrowing just to survive, repaying only to fall short again.

We had no room to save. Our budget barely covered our needs—and left nothing for our wants.

But I kept walking. To school. To church. To wherever my dreams whispered, *keep going.*

And maybe that was the miracle of it all—that even surrounded by debt, I was quietly learning how to invest in something deeper: faith, purpose, and vision.

Walking Barefoot Towards Destiny

College came like a door cracked open—not wide, but just enough for me to squeeze through with faith and family pushing me forward.

Thanks to the relentless support of my siblings, I was able to enter one of the top universities in the Philippines. I pursued a degree in Business Administration, majoring in Marketing. It felt like a dream I never dared to say out loud. I even served as the President of our Junior Marketing Association—a role that taught me even more leadership, confidence, and how to carry a vision with both humility and integrity.

With a clear goal in my heart and determination in every step, I gave it my all.

I was ready to finish strong.

But just when I thought I was nearing the finish line—life threw me one final test.

During my final semester, everything came crashing down. My family could no longer support my tuition. I was just a few steps away from graduation—and suddenly, I stood at the edge of uncertainty once again.

I remember whispering to myself, *"I'm almost there... now is not the time to give up."*

So, I didn't.

With trembling resolve, I stepped into a new role: a working student. I applied as a fast-food crew member—I landed a job as a fast-food crew member—serving smiles and meals at Greenwich, and even had the privilege of spending time working at the iconic Jollibee.

I worked the morning shift from 8 a.m. to 2 p.m., then rushed to school where my classes ran from 3 p.m. to 9 p.m.

With only one hour between my shift and my first class, I had just enough time to change uniforms, reset my mind, and start again—from worker to student, from exhaustion to determination. Every day, I walked nearly 500 meters—barefoot—under the sweltering Manila heat, crossing the busy highway bridge, drenched in sweat and soreness. My muscles ached, but I pressed on. There was no other way.

Each step was a reminder: *this isn't easy, but it's necessary.*

Still, I didn't stop there.

To meet my sales quota and earn a little extra, I pitched food orders to my professors—right in their faculty rooms. From my workplace, I would come to school and I would collect their orders, rush back to the fast-food branch, process everything, and return just in time to deliver each meal before class.

Every single day, that was my routine.

It wasn't glamorous. It wasn't easy. But it was what kept me going.

But even in the midst of the grind, I faced obstacles beyond physical exhaustion.

My 8 p.m. to 9 p.m. class in the Franchising course was especially hard to keep up with. Exhausted from the day, I often struggled to stay awake. And during the first weeks of the semester, I occasionally dozed off in class. My professor, being a professor, would call me out for recitations everytime she would catch me asleep. Of course, I couldn't answer. And so she failed me in the preliminaries.

But instead of breaking down, I rose.

I poured even more effort into her subject. I stayed awake, I studied harder, and I eventually passed both midterms and finals. That small victory meant everything.

One of my other professors, who knew about my situation, offered me another opportunity—to work as a dorm caretaker. In exchange, I was given a free place to stay near campus and a small allowance. I accepted without hesitation. It meant I could finally stop commuting from the province to Manila. It also meant scrubbing floors, collecting payments, cleaning toilets—but I didn't mind. Every task was a step closer to my dream.

Fast-food worker by day. Student by night. Dorm caretaker around the clock. I carried it all just to finish that final semester.

There was one night I will never forget.

I was reviewing for an exam, eyes fixed on my notes, but my brain refused to cooperate. I was too tired. Too drained. I knew I was good at memorizing—it had always been my strength. But that night, nothing would stick.

It was past midnight. I still have work the next day. I needed to pass my exam. Yet, my body was drained. My eyes blurred with tears.

"Lord," I cried, "I don't know what to do anymore."

There's nothing I can do but cry for the next minutes. I played worship music softly and whispered a prayer through sobs, surrendering my tomorrow into His hands.

I didn't finish my notes. I didn't cram. I just let go—and slept.

And true enough, in that moment of weakness, He became my strength. He took control of the situation.

I passed that exam.

"The Lord will fight for you; you need only to be still." – Exodus 14:14

Then came one afternoon I will never forget. I had just come from work, exhausted and drenched in sweat, when I walked through the gates of my university. For a moment, the world slowed down. It felt like a movie scene.

I watched my classmates laughing, chatting, studying, untouched by the burdens of the world that I carried at the early stage of my life.

And in that brief, quiet moment, I looked around and made a vow in my heart:

"One day, I'll return here—not as a student, but as a professor."

And I tucked that promise into my heart like a seed waiting to bloom.

Then, finally—graduation came.

And beyond that, I was deeply honored to be awarded as the Best Marketing Student—a rare distinction reserved only for the most outstanding achievers. In fact, the award wasn't even given annually, making the recognition all the more meaningful. To be chosen was both humbling and unforgettable.

I stood there, diploma in hand, heart pounding, eyes filled with tears.

I made it.

I made it not by luck—but by God's grace.

With blistered feet. With tired hands. With sleepless nights.

But also, with a God who never left me, a family who held me up, and a dream that refused to die.

That diploma wasn't just paper. It was a solid stone—the first firm step toward the life I had always dreamed of building.

Chapter Two: Planted for a Purpose

How Faith Built the Woman, the Business, and the Mission

The Thread That Held It All

As I look back on the road I've walked, I realize that the thread holding everything together—through every hardship, heartbreak, and breakthrough—has always been my faith.

My background as a Christian didn't just help me survive the storms; it gave me the strength to walk through them with hope. My parents, despite all our struggles, raised us with reverence for God. And even when life was hard, they made sure our hearts were soft—anchored in His love, grounded in His grace.

It was this foundation that held me when everything else felt like it was falling apart.

Even as a child, I believed deep down that the Lord had bigger plans for my life—even if I didn't understand them yet.

I remember those scorching summer days, when a local born-again Christian church would host a children's Bible camp right in our neighborhood. It was the highlight of my year. For a few precious days, I was just a child—laughing, playing, eating warm meals, and listening to Bible stories told with joy and love. It was a sacred escape from the chaos at home.

Those summer camps didn't just feed my stomach—they fed my soul.

They reminded me that God saw me. That I was not forgotten.

One Sunday morning, when I was just seven years old, the pastor called the children to the front of the church for prayer. I stood there as he prayed over us. That was the moment I gave my life to Christ. I didn't fully grasp the weight of that decision at the time—but something in my spirit shifted.

From then on, I knew I belonged to Him.

And even at that young age, I clung tightly to one verse—a verse that would carry me through every valley:

> "For I know the plans I have for you," declares the Lord,
> "plans to prosper you and not to harm you,
> plans to give you hope and a future."
>
> —Jeremiah 29:11

That verse wasn't just a memory verse to me. It was a lifeline. A promise. A prophecy.

A Love Written in Prayer

In following God's path for my life, I've always believed that obedience would eventually lead to true success—not just in career or finances, but in relationships, peace, and purpose. And one of the most important decisions that shape that path is choosing the right partner—someone who doesn't just walk beside you, but walks with God too.

During my youth, I was actively involved in our church. I eventually became a youth leader in our community, guiding others while deepening my own relationship with the Lord. It was through these church gatherings—especially the major youth events and outreach activities—that I met someone who would later become my greatest partner in life.

His name was Michael.

At that time, he was the leader of the school outreach ministry. Driven, passionate, and deeply rooted in faith—we clicked almost instantly. We bonded over our shared love for business, entrepreneurship, and serving the Lord. In fact, before we ever talked about love, we became business partners. We sold newly released gadgets and popular items, sharing ideas, strategies, and long conversations about faith and innovation.

We were solid, steady friends for six years.

Then, intentionally, we began to pray for each other. Not out of impulse, but out of reverence. We wanted to be sure. We didn't want to start unless it was in alignment with God's will.

And so we waited. We prayed. We asked. For nearly a year, we sought God's confirmation.

Then, one day, we decided to take a step of faith—but in our own special way.

We planned three consecutive dates. For each one, we would bring each other a handkerchief. We used to collect handkerchiefs with embroidered cartoon characters or designs, and the challenge was simple: if we brought the same design on all three dates, it would be our sign from God that we were meant to be.

On the first date—we matched.
On the second—we matched again.
Then came the third.

That day, I couldn't decide which design to bring. I had accidentally bought two different handkerchiefs and didn't know which one to choose. At the last minute, I randomly grabbed one and tucked it into my bag.

When we met, we smiled, knowing this was the final match.

He handed me his gift—and to my amazement, it was the exact same design I had chosen. Out of the two I had, I had picked the one that perfectly matched his.

In that moment, I knew.
We knew.
It was more than a coincidence.
It was confirmation.

God had written this chapter long before we arrived at it.

And that's how love found its way into my story—not rushed, not forced, but faithfully led by prayer, patience, and purpose.

God knew that the road to building a successful business wouldn't be one I could walk alone. So, in His perfect timing, He brought me a partner—someone who shared not only my drive and vision but also my unwavering faith. Together, we laid the foundation for something greater than either of us could've built on our own.

When Faith Meets Freight

Four years after our love story began, in the year 2012, we found ourselves preparing for two of the biggest milestones of our lives—our wedding day, and the birth of our very first business.

While most couples were busy choosing flowers and finalizing guest lists, Michael and I were also knee-deep in permits, legal registrations, and business planning. It was chaotic. Stressful, yes—but also deeply exciting. One moment we were reviewing caterer menus, the next we were finalizing corporate documents for what would become our first international freight forwarding company.

The idea of starting a business had always been in the distant plans—something I imagined doing in my 30s. But at just 27 years old, I wasn't sure I was ready. After six years of experience in the logistics industry, I had built strong connections and learned the ins and outs of sales and operations. Still, taking the leap felt terrifying.

But Michael believed in me.

He reminded me that timing isn't always about comfort—sometimes, it's about calling. He believed in our skills, in our teamwork, and above all, in God's hand over our lives. So I took a deep breath, said yes—to him, to the dream, and to the unknown.

And that's how Mega Mile Trans International Cargo Services, Inc. was born.

The early years of the business were far from easy. It was the planting season—one that required sacrifice, sleepless nights, and unshakable faith.

There were moments when we urgently needed capital to cover shipments. I remember the tension in the air, the weight on our shoulders. And just when we thought there was no way out—God would send an angel investor to bridge the gap. Again and again, His provision arrived right on time.

We made countless client visits, knocking on doors, introducing ourselves, and sharing what we had to offer. Earning trust in the logistics industry is no small feat. After all, we weren't just handling documents—we were entrusted with people's cargo, their livelihoods. Reliability wasn't just a promise—it had to be proven, every single time.

As the business grew, so did the challenges. We needed more capital, more manpower, and more refined systems. Managing people in such a demanding industry was no small task. The pressure was constant, the pace unforgiving. But we learned—often the hard way—how to build a foundation not just of structure, but of integrity.

We worked on establishing clear processes and service flows, building a culture of accountability and excellence. And when issues arose—such as shipment delays beyond our control—we had to face the difficult task of explaining the unexplainable to our clients. It tested our grace, our patience, and our communication.

But through it all, we pressed on.

There were nights when we barely slept. Days when the numbers didn't make sense. Weeks when everything felt like a balancing act between faith and fatigue.

But we had each other. We had our team.

With Michael leading our team and nurturing our people, and me handling clients and partnerships, we carried the vision side by side. In operations, we worked hand-in-hand, not just as business partners, but as husband and wife anchored in prayer and purpose.

The problems never stopped—but neither did our growth. And every challenge became a stepping stone toward something greater.

Our story isn't about overnight success. It's about commitment, courage, and a God who builds with us, brick by brick.

Because when you plant with faith, water with hard work, and protect it with love—growth is inevitable.

And we're just getting started.

Success That Multiplies

As I write this in the year 2025, I can hardly believe it's been nearly thirteen years since Mega Mile Trans International Cargo Services, Inc. was born from a vision, a prayer, and a leap of faith.

What began with just the four of us—my husband Michael, myself, and our two trusted partners—juggling client meetings, logistics paperwork, and countless sleepless nights, has grown into a thriving business with nearly 100 employees, moving close to 12,000 container shipments each year.

From zero clients, we now serve an approximate number of 50 clients, and that number continues to grow—not just in size, but in trust.

In 2014, we expanded our reach with our first international branch in China.

In 2023, we strengthened our local impact by opening a branch in Davao, Philippines.

And this year, in 2025, we reached another milestone—expanding the MM Group of Companies, which now includes Mega Mile Brokerage Inc. and Mile Movers Logistics Inc., alongside Mega Mile Trans.

Each step of this journey has been marked not by comfort, but by courage.

Not by coincidence, but by calling.

Not by our own hands alone, but by the gracious, guiding hand of God.

God is real. God is good. God's Word is alive.

As our hearts overflowed with gratitude, it became clear to us that this success wasn't meant to end with us. It was meant to flow through us.

With that conviction, we turned our focus toward giving back—not just in moments, but as a mission.

Through our company's corporate social responsibility programs, we've launched heartfelt initiatives aimed at serving and uplifting our fellow Filipinos. These include bag-giving caravans to empower young students, grocery donations to support families in struggling communities, visits to orphanages, aid for cancer patients, donations, and disaster relief operations in times of crisis.

But deep inside, we knew there was still more to give.

And so, in this same breakthrough year of 2025, we officially launched a dream that had long lived in our hearts:

Mission Miracle Foundation.

It was a vision that first took root in Michael—a desire to institutionalize our outreach, to widen our reach, and to become a consistent source of hope for others. The moment God opened the door, we walked through it with full hearts and willing hands.

Mission Miracle Foundation isn't just an extension of our business—it's an extension of our calling.

It exists because we believe that to whom much is given, much is required.

It's the living, breathing expression of our life mantra:

Blessed to be a blessing.

Because we are not just building companies—we are building lives, lifting communities, and living out God's goodness in every way we can.

Called to Secure Futures

While building our logistics company was a dream come true, another calling quietly found its way into my heart—one that would require not just skill, but compassion, courage, and conviction.

That calling was to become a financial consultant.

Having spent more than a decade in the sales industry, I understood the power of communication and trust. But more than that, I had a deep desire to use what I knew—not just to earn, but to protect. To educate. To empower.

So I took the exam and got my license as a financial consultant.

Soon after, one of my very first clients was a dear family member—a single mom with two young children. I encouraged her to take on a financial plan, not just for herself, but for the future of her kids. She agreed, trusting me to help her secure something stable for the years ahead.

And then, just four months later, the unimaginable happened.

She passed away suddenly due to cardiac arrest.

It was heartbreaking. I was shaken not just as a financial advisor, but as someone who deeply cared. I knew I had a responsibility—not just legally, but personally. I had made a promise. And I was determined to fulfill it.

Because her policy was still within the contestability period, the claims process became an uphill battle. For nine long months, I went back and forth with documentation, appeals, and follow-ups—determined to fight for the benefit her children deserved.

And then, finally, by God's grace,

Her claim was approved.

Her two young children—now in the care of their grandmother—were granted 6.7 million pesos.

It was in that moment that I fully understood my mission in this field.

This wasn't just another job.

It was a ministry.

A chance to bring dignity, security, and hope to people in their most vulnerable moments.

That single experience ignited something inside me. I knew I had to become more, to offer more—not for recognition, but so that I could reach more families with purpose, guidance, and compassion.

In 2023, I was named both Rookie of the Year and Agent of the Year nationwide in the Philippines.

In 2024, I earned the title again—this time, as a back-to-back Agent of the Year.

I reached not only the Million Dollar Round Table (MDRT) level, but also qualified for the Court of the Table and the prestigious Top of the Table—milestones only a few ever reach.

By God's grace and through the fruits of my hard work, my family and I were also blessed with all-expense-paid trips to some of the most beautiful places in the world—the United States, Europe, Australia, and the Middle East—as part of the global recognition for my performance.

But beyond the awards, beyond the applause, what fills my heart most is knowing that I said yes to the mission.

Because when you align your skills with your purpose, and your faith with your work, God opens doors you never imagined—not just for you, but through you.

That's why in every achievement I reach and every milestone I celebrate, I give all the credit to the Lord. None of this would be possible without His guidance, His wisdom, and the strength He gives me daily.

This journey—every success, every sacrifice—is not about me. It's about obeying the calling He placed on my life. I walk this path not for applause, not for recognition, but out of love and reverence for the One who called me.

"Whatever you do, work heartily, as for the Lord and not for men."
—Colossians 3:23

No matter how difficult the road becomes, I hold onto this truth: I am not doing this to impress people, but to live in obedience to my purpose. I am His follower. I am His servant. And all that I do, I do for Him.

And with every life protected, every family supported, and every dream made possible—I am reminded:

This is not just business.

This is calling.

This is kingdom work.

The Four Drivers Of Destiny

Now, you may be wondering—why am I sharing all of this with you?

Because whether you're a business leader, a dreamer, or someone simply trying to find their footing in the chaos of life, one truth remains: we're all striving for growth, for improvement, and ultimately, for impact.

And if there's one thing my story has shown, it's that success isn't accidental.

It's intentional.

It's cultivated.

And it's driven.

That's why I want to share with you the Four Key Drivers to Success—the very pillars that anchored me through the storms and propelled me toward every breakthrough.

You've heard parts of my journey—the poverty, the pain, the pursuit, and the purpose. And now, you'll see how these four drivers shaped it all.

Desire gives you the dream.

Every story begins with a spark—a longing for something more.

For me, it started in elementary school. A little girl, often hungry, sitting in a dark room lit by borrowed electricity, wondering if life could be better.

And in that wondering, something ignited—a desire not just for survival, but for transformation.

Not just for myself, but for my entire family.

Desire was the seed. The fuel. The beginning.

It whispered, "There's more to life than this—and maybe, just maybe, you can be the one to find it."

Decision gives you direction.

Desire alone is not enough. Dreams without action are just wishes.

At some point, I had to decide—not just to hope, but to move.

So I started small. In elementary, I made and sold handmade envelopes. In high school, I partnered with a neighbor to sell pillows. By college, I was juggling a fast-food job while studying full time.

These weren't random hustles. They were conscious decisions—each one a step closer to the life I envisioned.

I didn't always have clarity, but I always chose to move forward. And in doing so, I found direction. The path became clearer not because it was easy, but because I kept walking.

Determination gives you stamina.

The journey will be hard. What keeps you moving is not ease—it's resolve.

Growing up fast wasn't a choice—it was a necessity. The world showed me its harshness early on, and I had to face it with courage beyond my years.

There were countless moments I could've given up. Days when I was too tired to study, too broke to eat, too overwhelmed to try again.

But I remembered my why.

I remembered that little girl who once dared to dream—and I held on to her hope.

Had I stopped working part-time to pay my tuition, I wouldn't have earned my degree. Had we given up during the early years of our business—when the odds were against us—Mega Mile and the Mission Miracle Foundation wouldn't exist today.

Determination wasn't just helpful. It was essential.

Dedication gives you the victory.

Success is not won in grand gestures, but in consistent, faithful action—day after day.

Success doesn't come from a single moment of brilliance—it comes from showing up, over and over again. Day after day. Prayer after prayer. Choice after choice.

Staying dedicated to my values, to my purpose, and most of all, to the God who called me—that made all the difference.

There were moments that tested that dedication, especially when the easy way looked tempting. But one wrong move could've cost everything. So, I stayed anchored.

Like the time I fought for my first client's life insurance claim—a process that took nine months of effort, paperwork, and relentless follow-ups. It would've been easier to let go, but I stayed the course.

And in the end, it was worth it.

Her children were secured. Her legacy was honored. And my mission took a deeper root..

These are not just motivational phrases. They are practical truths—tools that help us build not only stronger businesses, but also stronger communities, families, and global partnerships.

I'm also sharing this for another reason close to my heart—to encourage and uplift fellow women in this industry.

Being a woman in a male-dominated field isn't easy. We juggle expectations, responsibilities, and battles that often go unseen. But I stand here, proudly, with every woman who dares to balance motherhood and momentum, who chooses to be both nurturer and nation-builder.

For me, the challenge was real.

While building a company, I was also building a family.

While raising two children, I was also raising capital, building teams, and serving clients—all while beginning a new chapter as a financial consultant.

It wasn't easy. It still isn't.

But it's absolutely possible.

And if my journey can show anything, it's this:

You don't have to choose between being a mother and being a leader.

You can do both.

You can thrive in both.

And in doing so, you'll become a beacon for others who are quietly wondering if they can do the same.

So to every woman reading this, to every leader, every dreamer—keep rising. Keep inspiring. Keep building.

The world needs what only you can give.

The Different Ending

And today, as I look back—from scavenging for torn books to standing on global stages,

From nights spent crying in silence to graduating with honors,

From hunger that hollowed our stomachs to building companies that now feed others—

I see one thing clearly:

God has been faithful to every word He spoke over my life.

Through it all—the valleys and victories—I've come to understand that success is not measured by titles or trophies, but by obedience.

By walking in step with the One who created me.

By knowing Him, trusting Him, and choosing every day to follow His ways—no matter how winding the road.

All that I am, all that I've achieved, all that has unfolded—it's not because of me.

It's because of Him.

And so I return all the glory, all the praise, all the recognition—to my Creator.

Because this is no longer just my success story.

This is my Jeremiah 29:11.

Poverty was never the end of my story.

Pain didn't get the final say.

Because God had written a different ending—one filled with purpose, peace, and possibility.

And the most beautiful part?

He's not done yet.

Your journey may be different from mine. Your trials, your timeline, your terrain—uniquely yours.

But know this: if God can take a little girl with nothing but faith in her pocket and hope in her heart, and raise her into a woman building businesses, empowering others, and changing lives—

He can do it for you too.

So hold on. Press forward. Trust the process.

Because when God writes your story, it always ends in redemption.

And that… is only the beginning.

Author's BIO
Michelle Moreno

Co-Founder & President, Mega Mile Trans International Cargo Services Inc.

Vice Chair, MM Group of Companies | Award-Winning Financial Consultant | Faith Mentor

Michelle Moreno is a multi-awarded entrepreneur, sales leader, and faith-driven mentor. As Co-Founder and President of Mega Mile Trans International Cargo Services Inc., she helped grow a four-person startup into a multi-branch logistics group trusted by global clients—proving that vision anchored in prayer can move mountains.

Michelle also leads as Vice Chair of the MM Group of Companies, including Mega Mile Brokerage Inc. and Mile Movers Logistics Inc. In the financial services industry, she's an award-winning consultant under Pru Life UK Philippines—earning back-to-back titles as **Top 1 Financial Advisor nationwide in 2022 and 2023**, followed by Top 7 in 2024. She is a proud qualifier of the **Million Dollar Round Table (MDRT)** three times, **Court of the Table (COT)** twice, and the elite **Top of the Table (TOT)**—a rare distinction that marks her as one of the world's top financial professionals.

Beyond business, Michelle's heart beats for impact. As Project Director of the Mission Miracle Foundation, she leads initiatives that serve underserved communities with love, dignity, and hope. A ministry leader at Jesus Is Lord Church Worldwide, she walks in her calling to help others grow not just in success—but in spiritual depth.

Michelle is also a proud wife, mother of two, and believer that purpose and business can go hand in hand. Her journey is proof that you can build with integrity, lead with compassion, and rise with God at the centre.

Facebook: https://www.facebook.com/michellemoreno.ph

Chapter 4
Building The Leader In Me
A journey of hard lessons and growth

Sam Yauner

Prologue

For as long as I can remember, I believed I would one day become a successful businessman. Not in a cocky way, it was just a feeling deep down. I have no idea why I had that feeling growing up, I hadn't ever been taught to strive for it, it just sat there inside me. My grandma used to remind me that when I was a kid I would tell her that when I was older my chauffeur would pick her up in my Rolls Royce. But I didn't have a plan of how I would do that, or the industry I wanted to be in, I just had this unshakable belief that somehow, it would happen. That belief gave me a kind of freedom in my younger years. I drifted through school and early jobs with a happy-go-lucky mindset, safe in the assumption that things would eventually fall into place. What I didn't realise then was that the biggest obstacle to success wouldn't be finding the right job or the right industry, it would be me.

Chapter One: Am I Built for This?

There was a heatwave in July 2019, and as someone who cycles to work, I had to swap the guarantee that I wouldn't get soaked in rain for the guarantee that I would be drenched in sweat. Some trade-off. I was an all-weather cyclist anyway, so this was normal to me. I found cycling to work and back was my only respite – a time that I treasured as the only time in the day that I had to myself. 30 minutes to clear my head, 30 minutes to transition from husband and father of three to CEO of a roller coaster logistics business.

My route took me straight down Green Lanes, past the impressive collection of Turkish restaurants, up the steep climb to Manor House, down the hill past Clissold Park, and past the end of the road where I grew up. Quickly round Newington Green and the housing estate that I was so terrified of as a boy, and then 5 minutes later, I'd arrive at the office. We had a space in a communal building nestled to the side of Shoreditch Park, and we had just moved one floor up, mercifully to a space that now had air conditioning.

The daily cycle to and from work was nostalgic; I could practically see my old house as I raced by. Past the shopping centre where my Mum used to take me to buy new trainers, and past the road where my old primary school friends lived. I would go past the park that I had played in a thousand times, and past the shop that used to sell me beer when I was underage.

But July of 2019 wasn't a good month for me, and the nostalgia added to the pressure. My memories were of times filled with happiness and carefree living. There was no responsibility back then, and I was looked after – someone else was making sure I was OK. Now the roles were reversed. It was me that was providing for a family, me that was leading a business, and those memories of happy times made me yearn for it again. Where would our money come from if the company folded? How would I pay back our loans? Would I lose our house? Could we afford to stay in London? How do we secure more customers? Do I have to go to China again? How much more of my kids' childhood do I need to miss? How can I provide for them? I want this to be a success, I'm 10 years in. Why is this so hard? How many more times can I arrive at work with a smile on my face, be there for my team, lead by example and bring the energy? I was broken.

Then one morning in July, I left the house to go to work, got on my bike and headed down the usual route. By the time I passed the shopping centre, I realised I had no memory of the first part of the cycle; my head was full. Past the Turkish restaurants, my sight started to become cloudy, and the sounds of the road became muffled. Up the hill to Manor House, I hardly realised I was climbing at all. Finally, as I reached Clissold Park, I came to a stop. I wheeled my bike into the park and found the first bench I could, and I collapsed onto it.

The tears I cried that morning on that bench in Clissold Park felt like both a release and a warning. I couldn't go on like this. Battle after battle, being the one at the front who people looked up to, being relied on as a leader, being relied on as a provider. I had wanted to be that person so much, but it had become such a burden. The business was up and down, and my relationships with those close to me, both at home and at work, were not easy to navigate. I couldn't do it anymore.

I stayed there for around an hour, until I had calmed down a little, and then got back on my bike and continued my journey to the office. As I turned the corner into Penn Street next to Shoreditch Park, I put on my virtual coat of armour, and then I was there – back into battle, back to the same day that I had lived over and over for the last 10 years.

Chapter Two: Teenage Lessons

I was born in 1979 and grew up in Highbury, on the border of the boroughs of Hackney and Islington, in a large Georgian terraced house. My Dad was a self-employed architect, and my Mum was a teacher in the local borough. I have one brother, three years younger than me.

Our house was so close to the stadium that in the summer, if we had the back windows open, we could hear the crowds cheering for Arsenal. In the late 1980s, my primary school was located on a road adjacent to the old Highbury Stadium, and the players would walk past at lunchtime while we were in the playground. They would come back holding their fish and chips, and we'd kick the ball over the fence so that they would kick it back to us whilst we sang their names.

I attended a private secondary school, made possible by contributions towards my fees from my grandfather and my uncle David. David was a mild-mannered man married to my dad's sister. He was a very successful businessman in his own right, and we would see him, my aunt, and my cousins a few times a year. I wasn't fully aware back then of how much he was helping my parents with the fees, and every time I saw him, I found it quite awkward to speak to him.

From my house in Highbury, the secondary school that I went to was a forty-five-minute drive out to the border of Essex. I took a school bus there and back six times a week (yes, we had school on Saturdays), and it was very sports-focused, which I loved. Around 20 pupils were coming up from inner London every day, but most of the pupils at the school came in from Essex. From the outset, I felt disconnected from them; they were not the type of people that I was familiar with. Most of them oozed wealth. New trainers were important and lavish holidays were spoken about; they all had the latest sports kit, and their parents had fancy cars. I felt pretty out of place, but never to the point of making me unhappy. It was school, it was where I was, and I never questioned it.

I coasted through the first 5 years of school without putting much effort in and my Mum gave me the nickname Mr Minimum. My GCSEs turned out OK, and I fooled myself into believing that the same would happen with my A levels, but the opposite happened. Perhaps that school was no longer right for me, maybe I needed a change, but I stayed and I struggled. I spent the next two years just about getting by academically. I used to sneak out of the gates to smoke cigarettes during breaktime, and I started to skip lessons regularly. I ended up getting lectured by some of my more supportive teachers who, instead of disciplining me, tried to light a spark inside me and warned me that if I continued on the pat I was on then I would struggle to get decent grades: "You're better than this, you need to be in the lessons, you have what it takes". They were right, I kept doing it, and as they predicted, my final results were disappointing. Despite being a popular kid with many friends at school, I was happy to leave at the end of the year. I was totally fed up with education, I knew it didn't suit me, but I knew that it wasn't over. My teachers and parents had told me time and again that the next step was university, there was no other choice; secondary school had simply been the lead-up to that next phase.

I applied to study drama at university, the only thing left at school that I enjoyed, other than sports, but I was rejected from every course I applied for. It turns out that academic results made a difference for that too (who would have guessed). And so I left for my gap year, not knowing where I would end up, but knowing there was an expectation for me to continue in the system and try to obtain a degree.

I look back on my gap year as one of the most important periods in my life to date, building character and learning to fit into a different culture, a different way of life. I absolutely loved it. The lessons I learnt during that time have shaped me ever since; they permanently changed my lens, and I began to see others differently, treat people more compassionately, and carry a deeper awareness into every relationship and decision from then on.

I had chosen to go to South Africa and had secured a place as a teaching assistant in a primary school high up in the north of the country in a town called Tzaneen. The placement was arranged by an organisation that specialises in placing students across the globe in the year between school and university. I had signed up for a 6-month placement and planned to travel for 2 months afterwards. I was nervous about leaving the UK, but I was extremely excited about the prospect of the freedom I was about to experience.

My arrangements in South Africa meant that I actually lived on the site of another school, approximately 30 minutes away from the school where I was placed and where I would be working for 6 months. My accommodation was a small rondavel – a round hut with a thatched roof – with no decoration and containing just a bed and a fridge, with a bathroom to the side. I drove to the local town each morning down a mountain through a forest. We were an hour's drive from the Kruger Park and I couldn't have been in a place more different than my comfy townhouse in London.

I had never been away from home for so long on my own, and I was out of my comfort zone. This was my first true test of independence, and I had to learn how to adapt, function on my own, and rely on myself without the emotional safety net of family or familiarity.

After settling and living in the country for a few months, I had made lots of friends, both locally and at the school where I was working. One of the men I had become friends with was a farmer who I had got to know from frequent Friday night visits to the local village pub. One Friday, he asked me if I wanted to go with him the following day to find some more workers for his farm. He would pick me up at 6 am, and we would drive out to a local township about 2 hours away. Completely naïve and keen for any experience that came my way, I said yes.

The next day, I was ready at 6 am and jumped into the cab, sitting in the passenger seat of his pickup. Behind me, sitting in the tray at the back, was his head worker. We arrived at the township around 8 am, and the man in the back jumped out and went straight through the buildings and disappeared. We waited for approximately 30 minutes, and then the head worker re-appeared, closely followed by five men, all carrying bags over their shoulders. They jumped into the back of the truck and then without saying a word, my new friend drove away for the return journey.

As we drove our way back, I plucked up the courage to ask him who the five new men in the back were and what they were going to do when they got back to his farm. "Don't worry about them", he said, "I'm giving them a chance to earn some money", and that was all he said. I found out later that this was a common trip for him. When new workers for the farm were needed, my friend would drive out to the local township and send his head worker to round up some new recruits. There was never a shortage of men who wanted to come, and they would literally just pack a bag there and then, say goodbye to their families, and jump into the back of the pick-up. It blew my mind that a person could just up-sticks like that, say goodbye to their children in a heartbeat, and head off 2 hours away with little consideration. How desperate could they be? Was my friend doing them a favour, or was he taking advantage? It was an extremely complex situation for an 18-year-old to process rationally.

My time in South Africa made me acutely aware of the inequality and social divide in the country, and it left a lasting impact. I began to understand how deeply unfair the world can be and how privilege can shape, or distort, your understanding of it. My illusion of normality was shattered, and I started to recognise how insulated my previous experiences had been.

Looking back now, I can see that my journey in South Africa gave me much more than just incredible stories to tell. I had arrived open and eager; I was desperate to say yes to everything, but I left with the uncomfortable awareness that sometimes, good intentions weren't always enough. I saw how easy it is to become complicit in something, even when you're trying to help. And I saw how people can shape the truth to suit their narrative. It's so easy to convince yourself you're doing the right thing when really, you're just protecting your own comfort. It was the first time that I started to think that being a real leader may mean having to consider whether your own narrative is for the benefit of the wider group.

I realised what a privileged upbringing I had been given. There was food on the table; I had attended a good school, and we holidayed every year without fail. I grew up in a house full of love and support, and my parents had ensured that I had been given everything I needed to be a success, it was just up to me to use the platform I had been given to make sure it happened.

But I didn't.

Chapter Three: Pushed Onto The Right Path

It was the middle of September 1998, and I found myself in a car, sitting next to my dad, driving up the M1 motorway on my way to Sheffield to start University. I have no idea how he felt at that moment, but now that I have children of my own, I suspect he was filled with excitement and pride that his son was growing up and starting a new chapter in his life. I know how I felt, though – I wasn't too pleased about it. The expectation that I would go to university had become a reality, and rather than accept it as a natural progression, I had started to question why my path was being decided by other people.

Having been rejected by all the universities that I had applied to for a drama course, I had settled on Business Studies with French, whatever that is. My parents had sent me a dozen prospectuses whilst I was in South Africa, and I had decided, from the other side of the world and without seeing a single university or speaking to anyone about the courses on offer, that Sheffield was the one for me.

The first term didn't change much inside me. I felt out of place again, but this time not because of the people I was surrounded by; it was because of the life I was now expected to lead. More structured education (4 years!), more sitting in front of someone telling me what was what, more of me writing down what I had been told and accepting that this was 'learning'.

For the first term that I was there, I went to every lecture and I went to every seminar, I followed the routine that was expected of me, and I hated it. I felt overwhelmed by the buildings that I had to be in, the giant lecture halls were isolating, and I was unsure how to act in the seminars. It felt like everyone was protecting their own interests; information wasn't shared amongst the students in case it gave you an advantage. I had to try to find out where to register for X or how to apply for Y. There was no collaboration or teamwork. I felt alone and uncomfortable during the daytime.

The evenings and weekends, however, were a different story. I made friends easily and enjoyed a great social life very quickly. I joined a football team, started going to the gym, and quickly established the best places to go out at night. I loved the independence, and continuing to live away from home suited me. I was able to make my own decisions and be responsible for myself. I enjoyed the housekeeping aspect of washing clothes, cooking, and managing my finances, and I loved being able to come and go as I pleased, with no restrictions. This part of university life felt very natural to me; it was a shame that the educational side didn't.

When I returned after the Christmas break, I didn't attend a single lecture or seminar, and this remained the case until the end of the year. My housemates thought I was mad, but I was enjoying life too much without university to care. I had got a job at one of the biggest nightclubs in Sheffield, and walking out of my university accommodation to spend Friday evening behind the bar at one of the UK's leading drum and bass nights gave me far more of a thrill than I had ever had. Music, people, energy, money – this was what I was looking for. I was fully aware of what I was doing, but I never thought for one moment that I was doing anything wrong. I knew what the ultimate outcome of skipping lectures would be, but I carried on. I took out all the student loans that I could, and I continued to live my life in Sheffield, as an imposter in the city.

For some crazy reason, I decided to turn up to my end-of-year exams, and you can imagine how that went. Bar being able to write my name at the top of the page I was useless. I was called in to see the head of my course in the last week of the academic year, and I was told that I had failed the first year. My options were to re-take the year or to leave – so I told him there and then that I would leave. I went back to London that summer and didn't tell my parents and I returned to Sheffield for my second year 'at university'.

The second year was a mix of part-time jobs: events and silver service in the director's lounge at Sheffield United Football Club, more shifts at the night club and waiting tables at the Hilton hotel. But this time around, it wasn't as fun, and I had the horrible feeling of time just slipping away without any progress being made. It was a time that I don't look back on fondly because it was my first experience of slightly deteriorating mental health; however, I recognise now that this was a significant turning point in my life, and one that would ultimately lead to where I am today.

I called my parents and told them I wanted to 'quit uni', that it wasn't for me. They were as understanding as ever and supported my decision, and before I knew it, I was back alongside my Dad, driving back down the M1 to London, with no idea what I was going to do with my life. My parents welcomed me home on one condition: that I get a job. And so, literally the following morning, I left the house and walked into Islington to the local high road and promptly got myself a job in a bar called Pitcher and Piano. Little did I know at the time that Pitcher and Piano was to become my 'university'.

Working for Pitcher and Piano was undoubtedly the time that I found the path to become who I wanted to be. I started as a barman, quickly became Head Barman, and within 5 months, I had been put on their management training scheme and did a stint in the Soho branch to learn about the kitchen. My journey through the management academy took me to Dover Street in the centre of London, as well as Chiswick, where I served as Deputy Manager, and then to Bishopsgate in the city, located next to Liverpool Street Station. I was asked to travel around the country to various bars when cover was needed, doing a short stint in Reading and helping with the opening of the Birmingham branch. I spent most of my days in the bar, and my work and social life blended into one. I finally had some disposable income. Life was good.

I was surrounded by people that I could relate to and people that I could learn from. There were people I looked up to, and there were people who looked up to me. I enjoyed the busyness of the weekend trade and the buzz of a five-person deep bar, serving non-stop until last orders. There was the buzz of the relationship with the door staff, being their 'boss', wearing an earpiece and making decisions on who was too drunk to stay in the bar. I loved leading by example, getting stuck in and showing the staff that I was happy to be on the front line with them. If a glass were to smash, I'd clean it up. If a toilet was blocked, I'd sort it out. I'd make sure there was enough cash in the till and take out the notes if they were bulging out. Would the chefs like a drink? I'd get them a round of Cokes. The satisfaction of cashing up at the end of the night to see how much we had taken that day. Sitting with the team when the doors were closed and we had all finished, having a drink and talking about the events of the night. This was it, this is my world. Work hard, play hard, learn on the job, learn from others. I was in my element.

Being in the Pitcher and Piano 'Academy' meant spending occasional days training at head office and gave me the opportunity to go away on 'work trips'. We had a three-day team-building event in the Lake District, and we got taken to Barcelona by Bacardi. There were nights out with the suppliers and company Christmas parties. We networked and we built our own personal brands, to be known and to climb the management ladder. The area managers knew who I was because I made sure I made friends with them all. I used all of my natural social ability to show that I should be on a trajectory to the top, and it worked.

I had arrived early for a training session one day at the Hammersmith HQ and was upstairs chatting with one of the head office staff when I noticed a girl come through the door, a huge smile on her face, with incredible curly hair bouncing around as she hugged everyone and said hello. She was full of energy, and she immediately held the room. I discovered that she was a trainee manager at the Bristol branch and had recently joined the company. I introduced myself and we spent the rest of that day chatting, so I asked her if she wanted to come for a drink with me after the course had finished. We had a lot of fun that night and continued to see each other whenever she was in London. I used to send her silly messages on the fax machine from my bar to hers. Luckily for me, she got a move to the same London bar that I was in, and before long, we were officially dating, and then living together.

Today, my closest group of friends is made up of people that I met during those four years at Pitcher and Piano and out of that group, four are god parents to my children, one is my business partner and one of them – the one with a huge smile and incredible curly hair – is Kate, my wife and mother to our three children.

I built connections that will last a lifetime and established a leadership style that would later help me launch my career as an entrepreneur. That environment had taught me how to lead long before I ever called myself a leader, and it helped me understand the type of leader I wanted to be: one who consistently shows up, earns respect rather than demands it, and knows when to step in and when to step back. I learned how to read people, how to keep morale up, and how to make decisions under pressure. Those moments, standing alongside my team and solving problems in real-time, laid the foundation for the leadership style I still carry today. But it wasn't just about keeping the energy up; this was real business with real numbers. Every shift involved running an operation, managing people, providing customer service, and, of course, ensuring profitability. If you got something wrong, you felt it immediately, and that kind of immediate feedback gives you a steep and valuable learning curve.

Looking back, I wonder whether I should have left education sooner. University didn't suit me, and I was never motivated by coursework or theory. I was motivated by momentum, by the idea of building something, earning money, and eventually being someone that people would look to and rely on. In South Africa, I'd already experienced the kind of emotional and social education that traditional systems rarely offer, and perhaps that had hardened my resistance to the idea of formal learning even more.

The workplace, on the other hand, lit something in me that I hadn't found before: a blend of freedom and focus. I thrived when I could use my social skills to lead a team, deliver something real, and get paid for doing it. And for the first time, I felt like I had stepped onto the path I was always meant to follow.

I'd walked away from university, lied to my parents, and had very little to show for two years away from home. At the time, it felt like failure. But looking back now, I can see it differently. Leaving that path, or being pushed off it, was the moment my life began to take the direction that I had yearned for. I wanted to lead, I wanted responsibility, I wanted risk with reward, and I knew that this would be the route that I would take for the rest of my life.

Chapter Four: Trial By Co-Founder

Kate and I left Pitcher and Piano together at the beginning of September 2004 and embarked on an epic trip around the world. After a short 5-day detour via Hong Kong, we arrived in Cairns, Australia, to start a year-long work visa. We bought a blue and orange zebra-print van that had a bed in the back, and we drove around Australia, finding work wherever we stopped. We picked bananas, apples, butternuts, melons and watermelons. We drove into the middle of the country and headed south, hit Adelaide and Melbourne and spent a 3-month hiatus in Sydney, which saw us both return to the hospitality industry. Kate worked in a Japanese restaurant (and brought exceptional sushi home for us after the shifts in the evenings), and I was a removal man during the day and a part-time barman at night. We drove across the Nullarbor to Perth, and up the west coast. We stopped for another three months in a small town called Kununurra to pick fruit again and recharge our bank accounts. We finished our year back in Sydney, having driven 40,000km (equivalent to going once around the world). From Sydney, we flew to New Zealand for 2 months, then to Asia to visit Thailand, Cambodia and Laos and met up with my parents and my brother in Vietnam for Christmas at the end of 2005 having not seen them for over a year. We finished up with three months in India.

I picked up a stomach bug in Laos that I couldn't shake, and by the time we got to India, I had already lost a lot of weight. The Asia trip had been interspersed with trips to hospitals, where I tried, unsuccessfully, to get cured. So when I woke up in a small hotel bedroom in Rishikesh on my birthday in May 2006 and was too weak to lift myself, Kate decided enough was enough and she booked our flights back to the UK. We had been away for nearly two years, and it was time to go home. It was also time to start taking my career seriously and get back on track to start a business and become the successful entrepreneur I had always aspired to be.

Back in the UK, I breezed through a few different jobs, looking for an opportunity, worried that I might get stuck in hospitality again. Kate gave birth to our first child, Lyra, so I needed to earn a living; I needed something stable. I decided to give recruitment a try and landed a job at a large international firm. It was the first time I had to wear a suit to work. Having been placed in a department with an office in the centre of London, I started the most soulless 6 months of my life. It was a push to move to a 9-to-5 schedule, but boy, was it awful. I had been asked to move into the Contact Centre team, recruiting call handlers to work in call centres. Imagine trying to sound excited about selling the dream of a £ 15,500-a-year job to someone desperate for work; it was hideous. And I wasn't being paid too much more than them.

Christmas of 2008, and as the most recent hire, I had been given the honour of working over the festive period whilst everyone else took time off. I sat in the office alone, trawling job boards and newspapers, looking for job advertisements that I could call to see if they would accept a recruitment consultant to fill the position. I found an interesting-looking role for a business development manager at an equally interesting-looking company. This 'adult toy' company produced a range of prostate massagers as well as some other terrifying-looking devices. They positioned themselves in the market as a 'luxury brand'. I called them up and asked if they would be interested in me putting anyone forward for the role, and they asked me if I had anyone on the books who would suit it. "Errr, me?" I said.

So I ended up in a modern office in a cool part of town, just next to Tower Bridge, selling sex toys to wholesalers around the world. I was earning more than I was at the recruitment firm, and I was able to hone my sales skills. Soon, the actual product I was selling became irrelevant; it was the sales that mattered, and I loved it. I used to sit in the office until late at night, on the phone to the US, selling thousands of these things. It was a fun job, the team was friendly, and the owner had an aura about him. He had several businesses, drove a Porsche, and used to come into the office every day mid-morning and spend most of his time behind his desk on the phone. He'd take us for drinks on Fridays, and I'd ask him about his other businesses. His main business was warehousing, and he had a large distribution centre in Kent. He owned a vodka brand and a clothing brand, and had just done a deal to acquire a small cult men's retail chain that had several high street stores and was struggling. Lots of fingers in lots of pies, I loved it.

I sat opposite Doug, who had also recently started. He rated himself as a salesman, and there was a little bit of competition between us. The truth was that neither of us was doing as well as the company needed. It was six months after the 2008 financial crash, and the average consumer was broke. Funnily enough, when there is a cost-of-living crisis and people are trying to save money, the last thing on their shopping list is a luxury sex toy. So, despite the fun and the volumes we were selling (which I thought was pretty impressive), it wasn't enough to maintain the whole team, and Doug and I soon got the hint that we might be the first to go if it came to that.

Doug and I used to have lunch together, and we would exchange stories about our backgrounds and the jobs we had both had leading up to where we were today. One day, he told me about a business he used to work in where they sold shipping containers. Their customers were storage yards, building sites and importers or exporters who used a 'shipper's own'. It sounded interesting, and so, as the noises of job uncertainty grew louder, I dug a bit deeper. How many of these contacts did he still have? How quickly could we get this started? How much would we need to launch? He had the idea and the know-how, but could I find the money? I got caught up in the excitement of trying to start my own business and didn't give it much thought. We created a business plan (which contained no numbers, just a description of what we were going to do and how we planned to do it), and I called my quiet uncle David to see if we could come and pitch the idea to him.

Could this be the moment that I set myself on the way to being the entrepreneur that I always wanted to be? Should I really be introducing a guy I've only known for six months to my uncle to pitch an idea that I didn't know much about? Risk and reward, risk and reward. But how much of a risk was it? My only risk was that I might lose the money David put in, and I would be back to square one. How bad could that be? I've dug myself out before, I always do, but is this different? I'm a father now.

We went to see David. This was the most recent of several business ideas that I had dared to propose to him. It was the first time that he had taken me seriously – it was certainly a better proposal than the plan to open the café near Victoria Park that I had drawn up on a side of A4 which said things like 'Get some nice coffee' and 'pastries that other cafés don't serve'. He asked lots of questions, mainly about Doug – who he was, and what his background was. Just when I thought it had started to take a turn for the worse, he asked how much we thought we would need to get it started.

Doug and I were sacked on the Friday, and the following Monday, we launched Corten Containers Ltd. I was the director of my own company. We found a small office just south of London Bridge train station in Southwark, a 5-minute walk from Borough Market. The room was big enough for two desks facing each other, and a fridge. We took a trip into town to buy a few office essentials, two computers and a customary indoor plant. We got a phone line and we found an Indian web designer to build us a website for less than £500, which looked like a website built for less than £500. We invested in some stock through contacts that Doug still had from his previous job, and we used Google Adwords to advertise online. Then we sat there and waited for the phone to ring.

I felt uncomfortable from the start. We had spent a considerable amount of money on stock, my uncle's money, and there was nothing we could do other than wait. I felt totally useless and completely at Doug's mercy. Surely we could be proactive about it; there must be people we can sell these things to. How is the advertising going? Do we really just wait?

We did wait, and we slowly started to sell a few containers. I learnt about them reasonably quickly, and I became familiar with all the suppliers. Terminology was easily taken on board, and the few intricacies of the different shapes and sizes of shipping containers weren't complicated to understand. It was a simple business, not particularly challenging. You bought something for one price and sold it for a fraction less than your competitors. You arranged a delivery, and you were done. The margins weren't big, so it was a volume business; we need to sell a whole load of containers to cover the salaries that Doug had decided that we should be paying ourselves. But the economics started to look quite challenging – an easy sell, yes, but we had to sell a lot.

A couple of months in, I suggested that we get the website properly sorted out. I hated what we had; it looked too cheap (!), and the branding was awful. I called my friend Rob who I had got to know from my days at Pitcher and Piano and who had left the hospitality industry himself to learn web design and online marketing. We used to hang out quite a lot, he was a weapon on the dance floor and had trained as a ballerina at the Central School of Ballet. He agreed to rebuild the website for us and he came into the office from time to time to build the site from there so that we could provide feedback quickly.

Around the same time, I started to notice that money was being withdrawn in cash from the company account, nothing huge, a few hundred pounds at a time. I asked Doug about it, and he told me that he had withdrawn it because he had bought a container in cash from a contact of his that I didn't know. He said it was a good deal. I let it slide because I was worried about a confrontation, but I couldn't see where that container had been recorded as stock. I couldn't let it go, and it nagged me for several days. I bottled it up and didn't speak to anyone about it, and I felt completely twisted inside. Trust – when it's gone, it's gone. I had never really felt at ease around Doug, and I was now business partners with him. I had allowed him to steer the opening of the company, and he had insisted that things were done in a certain way, that we paid ourselves a certain amount, and that we bought certain equipment. All this, even though we were a startup on a limited budget, and it just didn't sit right with me. This was the moment that I needed to speak up. Get a grip, Sam. Don't let him take the piss; do something about it. Get over your fear of confrontation and say something.

I went to my Dad and told him about the situation I was in, and he gave me the confidence that I could deal with it. So, the next day, I confronted Doug. There was flat denial, and the situation blew up very quickly. he tried to turn it on me, saying that he couldn't work with someone who didn't trust him. But it was black and white, and I knew that the only conclusion to the situation could be either an admission and an explanation for why he had done it, or that he should walk. It was an awful week, and events escalated quickly, culminating in a meeting mediated by my uncle David.

That meeting ended with Doug agreeing to sell his shares back to me and David at a cut price and he stormed out of the door with a final parting shot "I'm sorry Sam, but you just won't be able to do it, you can't sell and you're not a businessman".

I have used that moment as motivation ever since and have pinned it deep inside of me. A fire was lit, and it continues to burn to this day. I had confronted my fear of conflict, and I now had a choice: do I let this eat me up, close the business and go back to square one, or do I pull myself together and fight to make it work? I was fed up with dreaming. I had been doing it since I could remember, and now I had the opportunity laid out in front of me. Kate was pregnant with our second child, and I was determined. I had no idea what I was doing but I had been in those situations many times before and it didn't phase me. It was hugely exciting and terrifying at the same time. I could feel the pressure from the first second, but it was what I had always yearned for.

Chapter Five: War Dogs

And so it began, I walked into the office on the Monday as the boss of my own company. I was running a business for the first time in an industry I had never been in before. Fortunately, I had learnt the basics of the container sales trade, so I was able to continue, and that week I sold a few containers. I was confident that I would be able to do it. Rob came into the office that day, I had already told him what had happened with Doug in a call over the weekend, and he said that he would be happy to try to help if I needed it. He would come in to build the website, answer the phone and support me.

We were advertising online and we would receive enquiries through the website or by phone. We acquired a couple of regular customers, and we worked on a project to supply 20 containers to Celtic Manor for the 2010 Ryder Cup. We began to bring in new ' one-trip' containers from China, and we also undertook a project for the National Theatre, converting a container into a bar for them to use during their summertime festival. Rob stayed with me, and I managed to pay him a small amount that first month as well. The business was at least washing its face.

We regularly sold 'cargo-worthy' containers to customers for them to use for shipping overseas, and frequently we would then be asked to ship them. I had briefly looked into it when we first opened the business, but it seemed too complicated to handle, so I always turned down the opportunity and told the enquirer that we only sold the containers; they would have to use someone else for shipping. I had found a freight forwarder in Essex that had agreed to pay us a commission for referrals, so we pushed the enquiry to them instead.

One day, after hanging up on another shipping enquiry, Rob looked at me and said, "Why do you keep saying no to all these shipping enquiries?" I explained that I had looked into it previously and that it seemed incredibly complicated, and he simply said, "OK, you keep going, selling the containers to keep the company afloat, and I'll try to learn how to do it". We found two available domain names, www.weshipcontainers.com and www.weshipworldwide.com, and Rob built two basic three-page sites for both. We advertised those sites online and before long, we were fielding enquiries for shipping as well as enquiries to sell containers. Despite the challenge, it made perfect sense – there are only so many containers that someone will buy, but if you find a customer whose business is import or export, then you have infinite repeat business.

It wasn't long before we closed one. We had received an enquiry to ship a container to Mombasa, and we had spent the morning trying to work out how to do it "How about this one?" I had said to Rob, "MSC? Ever heard of them? They look like they ship there, and I think I've seen them before". We had received a quote which looked like it was written in a foreign language – BAF, CAF, War Surcharge – what on earth were all these things? Fortunately for us, MSC have a total at the bottom of their quotes, so we added a couple of hundred pounds, and I called the customer back and gave them our price. "OK, I'd like to go with that, please", he said. Shit! We booked the shipment and everything seemed to be going well until we received a call from MSC at 11:45 a.m. the day before it was due to sail. "Have you got the UCN?" the voice asked. "What's that?" I replied. "You need to clear the container and give me the UCN, the cut off is in 15 minutes and if we don't get it the container won't ship and you will get storage charges when it stays on the quay". "But this is an export", I protested, "it's just leaving the country, surely you don't have to use customs for something leaving the country". "Yes, you do," the voice said sternly. "Would you like us to do it for you?", "Oh, can you do that?" I said, "Yes, please!". And that was that, the container shipped – we had successfully arranged our first job as a freight forwarder.

From then on, it was full steam ahead, and we were soon reporting two revenue streams to David: Container Sales and Freight. Now, when I say 'reporting,' we were mainly getting lessons from David on how to prepare a P&L and how to read a balance sheet, and I suspect these sessions were fairly painful for him. We joined BIFA as an associate member, changed our email signatures and dropped the 'Containers' from the company name, we were now registered as Corten Ltd, and we ran two brands: Corten Containers and Corten Logistics.

The container sales continued; we upsold various additions to try to increase the margins. Our repeat customers continued to use us, and we closed some decent multi-container deals that injected much-needed cash into the business. Freight forwarding presented a steep learning curve. The two websites continued to perform well, and the freight side of the business began to grow slowly. Rob had been a key part in helping the business survive to this point and was in the office every day. He had changed our main website so we now had one site that promoted us as a freight forwarder and a container sales business, and we dived headfirst into learning about shipping. We were working as business partners, learnt together and made decisions together. He had helped when the business could have disappeared and had been a great support and driver on the freight side so I decided I had to cut him in, it felt right. We made a gentleman's agreement that when the time was right and the business had steadied, that he would receive the same share of the business as me, and I honoured that agreement a couple of years later.

We were deep into our 'War Dogs' era, posturing and blagging our way through our freight forwarding education; it was all smoke and mirrors. We took on the motto "the answer's yes, what's the question?" and we winged our way from deal to deal, learning all the while. Some of our customers paid the cost of our education, and we had to navigate some fairly difficult conversations with some angry customers… Instead of shipping a container from the UK to the US across the Atlantic, we managed to send it the other way around the world. The three-month transit time hadn't gone down very well with our customer when they realised what we had done. However, these mistakes were only made once. We learned from them, grew, and soon felt confident holding our own in conversations with customers and industry peers.

In those early days, we kept our secret close to our chest and utilised our customer service skills and ability to connect with people to expand our supplier base and acquire customers. We didn't feel like imposters as such, it was business and both of us felt we deserved to be there, and both of us were determined enough to scrap for survival. Neither of us were afraid of getting our hands dirty, and so we rolled up our sleeves and worked hard to become the real deal as soon as possible. It wasn't easy, of course. We covered every aspect of the business between the two of us, and I found it nearly impossible to switch off; the business lived in my head 24/7. I felt an enormous responsibility to make it work, both for David and for Kate. When Kate gave birth to our second daughter, Chloë, I took just one day off, something I now deeply regret.

David would check in regularly and we'd always tell him we were doing well. I kept up the same front for friends and family. I was enthusiastic and positive, painting a picture of the exciting journey we were on – and it *was* indeed exciting. But it was also a fight from the very start. I had battled to get to this point, and now I had to fight to make it work.

What I didn't understand back then was just how relentless the stress could be. How heavy the weight of it all becomes when there's nowhere to hide. And what I've learnt during this journey is that most business owners don't talk about their difficulties, it's taboo. Everyone says they're fine, everyone says business is going well. But what's going on behind the scenes? A lot of entrepreneurs are just trying to hold it together, and we were trying to hold it together more than most as we figured out what the hell we were doing. The pressure was constant, financially, emotionally and personally. I was learning about business the hard way: what compliance involved, how fragile and vital cash flow could be, how unpredictable people were, and how fast things could unravel if you weren't on top of it all. There were moments I seriously doubted myself, moments I thought we'd lose everything and moments when I thought we should give it up. But then there were sparks of clarity: the small wins, the first repeat customer, and the tiny signs that we were actually making progress. I was forced to make big decisions before I felt ready, but those early calls shaped the way I manage people and deal with pressure to this day. And through it all, I still showed up every single day, and I'm immensely proud of that.

Chapter Six: Why It's Worth It

It would be remiss of me not to dedicate a section of my story to my mental health, how it has suffered, and the battles that founders of businesses can face as they strive to create something that they have dreamed of. I've already told you about the day in 2019 when everything had come to a head for me.

What I've realised over the years is that nobody talks about what it actually feels like to run a business. Not properly. There's this unspoken agreement, especially amongst founders, that we all smile, we all say things are going well, and we carry on pretending we've got it under control. But underneath that, for many of us, there's something else going on entirely.

When I walked into the office that morning, after stopping at the park on my cycle into work, I didn't tell anyone what had happened. I didn't feel like I could; I thought being the boss meant being unbreakable and keeping up the facade. I was OK with showing emotion, and I have always worn my heart on my sleeve, but this was too much, and I didn't associate that with leadership at all. But over time, things have changed. I've since learnt how important it is to be honest about how you're feeling and to seek help if you need it. There's strength in that, too.

Looking back, COVID, for all the chaos and heartbreak it caused to many others, came at just the right time for me. Being forced to slow down and spend time at home, being with my family, and focusing on my health… I really needed that. I used that time to get fitter than I'd been in years, and I was able to reset both mentally and physically.

But this idea that business leaders should be machines is a myth. Social media doesn't help; founders screaming about how amazing they and their businesses are on LinkedIn is the norm nowadays, but I bet plenty is going on behind those posts. Perfectionism, for me, was slowly killing me. I've always wanted everything to be just right, and even now I find it hard to accept it when things aren't. Initially, I thought that anything less than perfection would be judged. That I'd be judged. But perfectionism is exhausting, and it stops you from trusting people. It forces you to micromanage, which can lead to the loss of great team members. And if you're the only one allowed to be good at anything, then your business becomes entirely reliant on you, which is ironic, because I've always said I didn't want to build a company that couldn't function without me.

You constantly question yourself, you wonder why you are doing it, you yearn for security and guarantees that you can pay yourself and others each month. You have people relying on you that you can not let down. You can see your physical and mental health suffering and you start to accept that this is just a consequence of trying to have a successful business. You get fooled into thinking that you should sacrifice yourself for the good of others – your family, your staff.

Letting go has been one of the most challenging but most important things I've learned. I've handed over entire parts of the business to other people, and guess what? They do it better than I. I've now learnt that that's not failure, that's leadership. Of course, with people comes responsibility. Ensuring everyone is paid and that they're happy in the workplace. And when you're putting everything you've got into building a company, it can feel overwhelming. The mental strain is enormous, and my sleep has suffered; it still does to this day. However, I now know my limits and play to my strengths. There are people on my team who are far better logisticians, better at IT, better accountants… and that's no bad thing! Are they perfect? No, but who is? What I bring is something different. Something less tangible, but no less valuable, and you know what? They always come to me for the final say, and they respect me as a leader in the group. I allow people to make decisions and ensure that the company culture, service levels, and tone are not compromised.

Now and then, something reminds you why you lead the way you do and why some of those sacrifices that you make are worth it. It was my birthday recently, and the team gave me a card. Nothing over the top, just a card. But the messages inside made me burst with pride more than any deal we have done over the years. They were about me as a person. "Thanks for always being there." "Thanks for the energy that you bring." "Thanks for believing in me and guiding me." It completely floored me. After sixteen years of this journey, it was the first time I felt truly seen. Not just as a boss, but as a human being trying to do his best. That card was just the latest reminder that I don't have to be perfect and I don't have to have all the answers. Leading with integrity and honesty, and doing so consistently, was what mattered. We have team members who have been with us for a decade – that's because of the culture in the business, and that's something that I can celebrate.

If I could say one thing to someone reading this who feels the way I've felt, it would be this: Bad days don't define you. Talk to people. Lean on mentors. Take advantage of people who have been there and done it. Take action when it matters, even if it's just a small step, the longer you leave something the heavier it weighs. The mantra I use and repeat to myself all the time is a line from a song from my favourite band: "Keep your head up kid, I know you can swim, but you gotta move your legs."

Chapter Seven: An Endless Education

We made a decision early on that if we were going to be a freight forwarder, we needed to look like one. We were also going to try to move faster than our competitors – our lack of red tape and the speed at which we could make decisions worked in our favour. That meant everything, from joining the correct associations to ensuring our website and tone of voice reflected what we were aspiring to be. We may have been learning on the go, but we were invested in it and did things correctly, which pushed us forward at speed. We joined BIFA, attended courses, and developed processes. We created shipping files, having never seen one before, and checklists to ensure we did everything we needed to do each time. We learnt about the requirements for different countries and the documents required for various types of cargo. We branched out into air freight (self-taught, of course!) and eventually became an IATA Cargo Agent.

This approach became part of our DNA. We wanted to be seen as a genuine option, as an established forwarder that could compete. And the more we learnt, the more convincing we became. But we had another aim – we wanted to stand out. We didn't want to just exist amongst the others, we wanted to be recognisable and without giving away our secret, we wanted to be different.

When Rob built our first website for Corten Logistics, he phoned me and told me he wanted the brand to be bright pink, and straight away, I loved it. We didn't want to blend in; we wanted people to remember us, and they did. Over the years, we've genuinely won business because someone remembered the "cool guys in pink". It became a talking point, and I would also go so far as to say a true reflection of who we were: bold, energetic, and a bit unconventional. We have pink walls in our office, and we even give away pink Corten branded socks to customers and partners as gifts. Our competitors were all blues and greens, with plain logos and predictable merchandise. We have pushed our brand, and it has reaped rewards. We continue to put a lot of care and attention into how we present our brand today; it's always been our identity.

We have also embraced technology from the start, and we went entirely paperless in 2014, which was ahead of the curve. That might sound obvious now, but back then it wasn't standard practice. We invested in freight software that allowed us to digitalise our operations and streamline communication. It wasn't just about going green; it was about being efficient, scalable, and modern. And looking back, it set us up to move faster than some of our competitors. We provided online tracking before most, and we were able to share documents with our customers digitally.

Then came our decision to embrace e-commerce. In late 2013, Amazon sellers and online retailers were knocking on doors trying to find freight partners. We received regular calls from sellers desperate for help. We were told that most forwarders had turned them away as they didn't want to work with Amazon, and the complexity of FBA put our competitors off. There was a feeling amongst other freight forwarders that Amazon were notoriously difficult to deal with and their conditions were complicated. The truth was they were just another warehouse with specific requirements for labelling and delivery into their distribution centres, which could be learned. We saw an opportunity and we developed it. We knew that being small meant we could be nimble and take advantage of this situation before others caught on.

We built a product for Amazon sellers and established a network of third-party warehouses worldwide. We offered our customers an end-to-end service, where we would ship their products from the manufacturers and then handle the warehousing for them through third parties. We increased our pallet count from 500 to 15,000 worldwide in just 6 months, and we offered high-margin add-ons like relabelling and repacking as an upsell.

We were unable to compete with the big boys for the large tenders, who would give little 4 year old Corten a massive freight contract after all? However, this was an opportunity to build a niche and establish a name, and we soon became known as the go-to business in the UK for Amazon and online sellers. It brought us business when others were slow to react, and it laid the foundations for long-term growth.

2015 was a big year for us. We'd just secured the largest shipment we'd ever handled, 265 tonnes of wire flown in from Dubai and India into the UK, then trucked to Hungary. At the time, we were still a relatively small outfit, and deals of that size didn't come along often.

Our freight business had primarily focused on direct customers, but we'd recently joined a freight forwarding network and found an overseas partner with offices in both countries to support the job. As (bad) luck would have it, the longer the shipment dragged on in the planning stage, the closer we got to our departure for the network's conference. We were about to manage the biggest deal of our careers, and we wouldn't even be in the country.

We found ourselves on the other side of the world in Qingdao. Our first time in China, attending our first-ever freight conference, where we pitched

Corten as a reliable UK partner to forwarders from around the globe, while 'the job of our lives' back home went ahead.

The bulk of the operation was being run by someone we'd only hired two months earlier, a Hungarian (coincidentally) with experience of logistics in her home country, but new to the UK industry and with no prior experience in air freight. It was a baptism of fire for her. We guided from afar, and she did a fantastic job. That shipment remains, to this day, the most significant single movement we've ever handled. We still talk about it, wincing slightly that we weren't in the UK to help out.

And our incredible Hungarian? She is now in one of our most senior and valued roles. Her journey through the business is one of the things I'm proudest of. Not because I take credit for her talent – she's phenomenal with unbelievable attention to detail – but because I remember sitting next to her when she started, correcting her English, teaching her the ropes, and watching her take it all in and run with it. She made the most of the opportunity, and I'm glad we were able to provide an environment that allowed her to flourish.

Joining that freight network did wonders for the business, and over time, we became members of several more. The unexpected upside was what it gave me personally: the chance to travel again. I'd travelled a lot growing up; my parents took my brother and me away regularly. I had my epic round-the-world trip with Kate, and I had my incredible gap year in Southern Africa. But I never expected this business to take me to the places it has when I started it.

To name a few, I've been to Singapore, Hong Kong, and Shanghai. I've been back to South Africa, across Europe, to Los Angeles and Miami, and more recently to Brazil, visiting Rio and São Paulo. We've met incredible people from every corner of the world. At every event, I'm reminded that our strongest asset, and probably mine and Rob's key strength, has always been building relationships. We enjoy it, we're good at it, and we work hard at it. Many of those trips have given us genuine friendships as well as long-term business partnerships.

My uncle David passed away in 2019. He had been living with Parkinson's for a long time, and I watched as it slowly got its grip on him over the years. It was a slow decline, and he was incredibly brave, never once complaining. Even as the condition took hold, he somehow always found the energy to come into our office once a month. He'd sit with us, go over the figures, ask questions and challenge us – never too direct and always in his own gentle way. And at every visit, he would take us out for lunch.

He never gave direct advice. That wasn't his style, he would ask questions instead. "Why do you want to spend that much, and what will the returns be?", "What happens if the deal doesn't come through?", "How will you fund it next month?". They were never confrontational; they were just designed to make us pause and think. He believed in us, but he wanted us to learn by doing, not just by being told. He helped us understand the mechanics of a business. How to read a P&L and how to spot warning signs in a balance sheet. He got genuinely excited when we landed a big customer, as if he were living the journey with us. And he was always there when we needed a boost, injecting money into the business more than once when cash flow was tight. He used to say, "I'll always back growth." And he did.

It was David who insisted that we get our shareholder paperwork done properly when we launched the business, hiring an expensive solicitor in Central London. At the time, it felt over the top, but he was adamant. "Prepare for the divorce before the wedding," he used to say. That paperwork turned out to be essential. When we needed to part ways with our original co-founder, it was the documents David had insisted on that allowed us to do it cleanly.

Growing up, he was my quiet uncle, calm, thoughtful and unassuming. But during the ten years we worked together, I got to know him properly, and what developed was one of the most meaningful relationships of my life. We grew very close, and I still miss him now. There are decisions I have to make today, and I often find myself wondering what David would say to help guide me.

The year he died, I created an award in his name: the David Kaye Award. It's our company's annual Employee of the Year recognition, given to someone who has truly stood out, not just for their accomplishments, but for who they are and how they consistently demonstrate their values every day. We have a board on the wall listing the winners, and David's name sits at the top. It's a small thing, but it means a lot to me and reminds me of where we came from and how his input helped us get to where we are today.

Chapter Eight: A Legacy Beyond Logistics

Our business is 16 years old, and we are in great shape. We are a team of 20 people, and we're posting the best results we've ever had. The team is made up of freight professionals from all over the globe who bring local knowledge and experience of their region to the business. Staff have come and gone but it's rare that we lose one and are disappointed about it, the good ones stay. We have team members who have been with us for 10 years, some for 9 years, and some for 8 years. The same applies to our customers; the churn is minimal. Everyone is treated with respect, we demand hard-working staff, and they are rewarded with a supportive environment and compensated above standard industry levels. Sometimes I arrive at the office to see a full room of people working away, saying good morning to me as I walk by, the occasional fist bump, a story about their weekend. It's the biggest reward I could have asked for. The team photo when we are off on a staff night out, the Christmas party, these are the moments that make me proud of what has been created.

The statistics were against us, but we've made it this far, and I have a good feeling that this part of my journey will end well. We don't hold any secrets anymore, and now we tell our story whenever we get the chance, with a huge amount of pride. We haven't done badly for an ex-ballerina and a guy who used to sell sex toys. We have proved that hard work and resilience are enough to succeed. We weren't lucky, we made our own luck. We made sure we were in the right place to catch the right cards when they fell. We took advantage of every opportunity we could, and we networked our hearts out. Some of the risks we took paid off, some didn't, but we learnt from our mistakes and went again, wiser, stronger, more determined than ever. Of course, I would like this chapter of my life to end with a financial reward, but ultimately, my goal is to see it through to a conclusion, that would be enough. I want my kids to tell their kids that their Dad had a company, he built it from scratch, and he created something that was a big part of many other people's lives. I want to have built something for others to look back on as their Pitcher and Piano moment, a place where they made life-long friends and memories.

Despite the challenges, I've genuinely enjoyed the journey: the learning, the people, the process of discovering what good practice looks like in a business. It's made me want to do it all again one day. Not necessarily in this industry, but somewhere I can utilise all the experience I've gathered and not have to start from scratch. I know what the early days feel like now, and I will be better prepared.

I've also found real fulfilment in mentoring and standing in other people's corners, helping them with their fight, and I think that's something I'd like to lean into more as well. I feel that this journey with Corten has given me the skills to one day move forward once again, whether that's starting another business myself or supporting others with their own ventures. But one thing is for sure – I'm not done with Corten yet. And until I reach the day where I can say that this journey is complete, I will continue to give my all.

In the 16 years of Corten, I've got married and had three children (Rufus, arrived in 2014). Rob have had our moments, but amazingly never really had a proper falling out. We've managed to turn a friendship into a business relationship and I wonder how many more entrepreneurial partnerships that started as friends have managed to last the distance? And whilst I'm proud of the way that I have moulded the company, I accept that the company has moulded me too. There is no doubt that I have changed as a leader and also as a person outside of the workplace as the years have gone by. I've become more boundaried and I'm more comfortable saying no. I have learnt that my hunch is usually correct and that caution is no bad thing; risks are exhilarating, however, untangling unnecessary problems can be draining. Take a bit more time. Consider your actions and ask for help or guidance if you need it.

I'm telling this story to offer a truthful account of what building a business really looks like: the highs and the lows. This is not a blueprint or a how-to guide, you could almost say it's the opposite. This is a story about learning, about fighting and about becoming a leader in my own way. I hope it helps anyone who has a dream but doesn't know how to get there. There are thousands of entrepreneurs who go under the radar and live normal lives, fight day to day and win the battles that are required to succeed.

I truly believe that with determination, application and the right morals, almost anything is possible. I've learnt that people, no matter where they are from and who they are, should be respected. And they in turn will respect you – and that's the foundations of a great team. After all, I would not be where I am today without the people who have been on the journey with me. Compassion is a strength. Make time for others, listen and be kind, you will be remembered for it.

Author's BIO
Sam Yauner

Sam Yauner is a **visionary leader, mentor**, and the **founder** and **CEO** of **Corten Logistics**, a UK-based freight forwarding company he launched in 2009. Without any prior experience in logistics, Sam built the business from the ground up through grit, resilience, and a deep commitment to learning and growth.

His leadership style is rooted in emotional intelligence, authenticity, and a steadfast belief that great companies are built by great people. Over the years, Sam has cultivated a values-driven culture where trust, integrity, and personal development are paramount. He is passionate about mentoring emerging talent, empowering individuals to unlock their potential, and inspiring others to lead with courage and compassion.

Beyond the boardroom, Sam is a devoted family man who treasures weekends supporting his three children at youth football games and cheering on his beloved Arsenal. He is proud to have created a company where commercial success goes hand-in-hand with community, lifelong friendships, and meaningful impact.

Sam is eager to share his insights and experiences to help others navigate the challenges of leadership and entrepreneurship. For mentorship inquiries or to connect, reach out at ✉ sam.yauner@cortenlogistics.com

🔗 https://www.linkedin.com/in/samyauner/
🌐 www.cortenlogistics.com

Chapter 5

Becoming Me
From Roots to Wings

Katharina (Kat) Attana

Chapter One: The Beginning of my Journey

A Dreamer's Lens on Life

I'm a dreamer at heart. I've always believed in fairy tales and happy endings—and even now, if a movie doesn't end the way I'd like, I ask my husband to come up with a better one just for me. That optimism is more than just a personality trait—occasionally an annoying one for others—it's the lens through which I see the world and the quiet compass that has guided many of my life decisions.

It carried me from a childhood in East Germany to new beginnings across the globe—from the U.S. and Hong Kong to eventually settling in Australia and finding my path in the world of logistics.

It's funny how things unfold sometimes. Looking back, there have been moments where it genuinely felt like the universe—or someone—was looking out for me. So, here's a little of my story—with all its ups and downs. It's been a journey filled with adventure, growth, and more than a few happy beginnings.

Childhood in the GDR

I was born on a crisp, sub-zero January day in 1982, under sunny, clear winter skies in Karl-Marx-Stadt—a city steeped in the routines and rhythms of the German Democratic Republic. That morning, my mum went to the local hospital alone. My dad, like many young men at the time, was away fulfilling his compulsory 18 months of military service. Childbirth wasn't considered a reason for leave, so he didn't meet me until I was already a few months old—and only saw me a handful of times until he completed his service when I turned one.

Life in the GDR was defined by scarcity, collective values, and a rigid structure—but also by community, safety, and simplicity. We didn't have a television for most of my childhood. My toys were handmade by my dad, mostly from scrap wood. I never tasted McDonald's until I was 18. And yet, I never felt I was missing out. I didn't know what I didn't have, and therefore, I never longed for it.

Evenings were spent reading, playing, or listening to the cadence of my parents' and grandparents' stories. It was a slower, more connected life. One of my fondest memories is of my great-grandma. She had an old oven covered in blue-green tiles and would rise at 5 a.m. to heat it with wood. I'd play nearby while she watched from the couch or told me stories from her childhood or fairy tales. My parents would later remind me of the outdoor toilet and how cold it was in winter—I don't remember that part. What I do remember is a childhood marked not by what we lacked, but by imagination and curiosity. I was one of those slightly annoying endlessly inquisitive kids, always asking so many questions.

Lessons from the Socialist System

Another aspect of my early years that left a lasting impression was the childcare and education system. Every child had access to state-run childcare, and it wasn't just about supervision—it offered structure, learning, and a deep sense of consistency. We remained with the same group of children and educators for several years, forming strong, familiar bonds. Our days followed a steady rhythm of music, outdoor play, and storytelling (we didn't have too many materials for crafts). At the time, it simply felt normal. But with the benefit of hindsight, I've come to believe it was one of the best early childhood systems in the world. It gave me a strong foundation and an early understanding of the value of community.

I still remember a visit from a group of Russian students—how they brought bread with salt, a traditional gesture of hospitality, and wore beautifully embroidered costumes. Looking back, it may have been a political exercise, part of the broader efforts to showcase unity among socialist nations. But that's not how it felt to me as a child. To me, it was a moment of cultural exchange, of colour and genuine human connection. It sparked my curiosity about the world beyond East Germany's borders.

Cracks in the System & Reunification

From the age of six, I was a proud *Jungpionier*. I wore my white shirt and blue scarf with a sense of ceremony during school assemblies. As Pioneers, we collected recyclables, sang songs, and helped one another. Each morning began with a call-and-response: "Für Frieden und Sozialismus – seid bereit!" and we would reply, "Immer bereit!"—*"For peace and socialism – be ready!"* – *"Always ready!"* Singing was a big part of our daily rhythm. I still remember the lyrics to songs like *"Ich trage eine Fahne, und diese Fahne ist rot"*—*"I carry a flag, and this flag is red"*—celebrating the red flag as a symbol of the workers, socialism, and the heroes who fought to end the war. Another favourite was *"Kleine weiße Friedenstaube"*—*"Little white dove of peace"*—a gentle, hopeful song calling for peace across all nations. Looking back, I realise how deeply those songs were woven with meaning. Years later, when my own kids joined Scouts in Australia, I smiled at the similarities—different uniforms, different values, but the same sense of community, ritual, and shared ideals.

Something else I learnt to value in hindsight – food. Food was simple, usually a little over-cooked, but healthy, made from whole ingredients—even if it was prepared in large communal kitchens. We ate what was seasonally and locally available: potatoes, eggs, cabbage, chicken or roast and occasionally spinach, though I only knew it as a green purée until much later when I realised it came in leaves. For dessert, we'd have stewed apples, grated carrots, pudding, or simply a piece of fruit. Christmas was special—we'd get oranges from Cuba and, sometimes, half a banana. I once saved mine for my dad, carefully tucked it in my school bag all day, only to find it squashed and brown by the time I got home. I was disappointed, but he ate it anyway, smiling, making me feel like I'd brought him a treasure. There was no fast food, no fizzy drinks, and no aisles of colourful snacks—but we never felt hungry. Meals were shared, and food was respected. It may not have been fancy, but it was enough.

I mentioned earlier my belief in something greater—a higher power, perhaps (no religion in East Germany). One moment in particular has stayed with me for life. It was a serious car accident. In the GDR, owning a car was a rare privilege. Ours—a basic Trabant—had hardly any safety features, but it gave us freedom. Both sets of grandparents helped buy it and used their connections to get one faster. Public transport between my dad's parents and our home took over ten hours. The accident occurred on one of those trips. One small mistake, a moment of distraction, and our car, with my parents and me inside, flipped three times and crashed into a tree. It was completely destroyed.

I lost consciousness and came to about 200 metres away from the car, with a woman running toward me. I hadn't been wearing a seatbelt. The roof must have come off, and somehow I was thrown clear. I escaped with just a small cut on my left wrist—shaped like a little wave. I remember the nurse jokingly asking if I wanted a "fun scar" taping two small Band-Aid strips in opposite directions.

My mum wasn't so lucky. She spent months in hospital. Despite the severity of her injuries, she made a full recovery. Both her knees were dislocated, her upper thigh bone completely shattered, and her hip broken multiple times. Her leg was saved by a very long surgery performed by a doctor in a small-town hospital near the crash site. Somehow, he not only saved her leg but also pieced the bone back together. More than 30 years later, when she needed a hip joint replacement, the specialists were amazed at the quality of his work. Most people would have lost their leg that day. That close call deepened my quiet belief in magic, and in the kind of hope that never shouts but always stays. At school, my class drew pictures for her, and my grandma used all her connections to get my mum a Walkman from an Intershop—the first time I heard about those special stores where you could only buy goods from the western world with western money.

What I remember most from childhood isn't what we didn't have—it's what we did. There was a strong sense of community. Neighbours knew one another. Kids played outside for hours, freely and safely. Healthcare and education were accessible and obviously excellent. My parents both worked full-time, but they never had to worry whether I'd be cared for or have something to eat during the day. Looking back now, I see that for what it was: a gift. A childhood that many children today might never get to experience.

But nothing stays the same forever.

While life in the GDR could appear idyllic from a human point of view—with its emphasis on community spirit, collectivism, and modest, structured living—it was, in many ways, a carefully constructed illusion. The socialist system presented a veneer of equality and security, but underneath, the economic foundations were fragile and the model was fundamentally unsustainable. The planned economy relied heavily on outdated machinery, bureaucratic inefficiency, and manipulated data to preserve the appearance of progress.

By the end of the 1980s, the truth was undeniable: the GDR was on the brink of collapse. Its GDP per capita was barely 37% of West Germany's, and its total national debt had ballooned to over 49 billion Deutsche Marks. More than 8,500 Volkseigene Betriebe (VEBs)—state-owned enterprises—employed around 4 million people. Many of these factories were technologically obsolete and grossly overstaffed, in part because full employment was a political mandate rather than an economic outcome. In some cases, factories employed two or three workers for tasks one person could have handled—just to keep the unemployment figure at zero. However, this "employment" masked stagnation rather than enabling prosperity.

Official productivity numbers were routinely manipulated to meet rigid five-year plan targets. There was little incentive to improve quality, efficiency, or innovation. Wages were largely decoupled from performance, and career advancement often depended more on party loyalty than competence. Creativity was not just discouraged—it was often penalized. Those who showed too much ambition or independent thinking risked political suspicion. Success could isolate you.

Meanwhile, a privileged political elite—party officials, senior bureaucrats, and Stasi-connected figures—enjoyed access to better housing, higher-quality goods, private clinics, and exclusive shopping outlets stocked with Western imports. While most citizens queued for basics like butter, oranges, or toilet paper, this elite quietly benefited from perks hidden behind layers of state secrecy.

The collapse of the GDR was not just political—it was economic, environmental, and institutional. Factories polluted rivers unchecked, consumer goods lagged decades behind global standards, and infrastructure crumbled. By 1989, the façade had cracked beyond repair.

After the fall of the Berlin Wall, the Treuhandanstalt—the trustee agency charged with dismantling East Germany's socialist economy—was formed almost overnight. From 1990 to 1994, the Treuhand oversaw over 6,500 company privatizations and nearly 3,700 liquidations. It was one of the most aggressive economic transitions in modern history. The result was catastrophic: up to 3 million jobs were lost, and the East German economy shrank by more than 30% within just a few years. Public assets were sold, often for symbolic sums, to West German corporations and foreign investors, many of whom dismantled local industries for parts or real estate. The total cost to the German state? Over 256 billion Deutsche Marks in losses.

As I grew older and began asking questions, I came to understand the deeper implications of my early experiences. It imprinted something in me deeply: the importance of numbers, of honesty in productivity, of measurable value in a functioning society. I saw that hard work meant little without process and accountability, and that inflated promises without economic substance inevitably collapse. My conclusion from this is clear: a government must care for its people, especially the marginalized, but it must also build a strong economy and set incentives for productivity. It's a bit like putting on your own oxygen mask first; only then can you help others.

Now, this was not just an economic transition—it was a social earthquake. The sudden shift to capitalism left entire towns without industry, identity, or hope. Once-proud workers found themselves unemployed and unemployable, their skills no longer valued. Pensioners lost their savings. Families split under the pressure of displacement and unemployment.

What a time to grow be alive! My family lived through this tectonic shift. In 1989, as East and West collided, our lives were rewritten. One of my grandpa's had spent 25 years in the army, sacrificing most weekends for duty, only to later discover that in West Germany, soldiers often went home by Thursday afternoon. My dad had just completed a PhD in philosophy—a field deeply tied to the ideological system of the GDR. Almost overnight, his qualifications became worthless. He found himself straddling two realities that no longer fit. But he didn't crumble. He picked himself up and did what needed to be done. He sold batteries, started a "re-education" business with a *Wessie*, and went back to university to get a business degree. Eventually, he found his true calling in the non-profit sector, where he became a regional director for a charity organisation. That role—grounded in service, purpose, and compassion. A great place for my dad!

My mum, who had studied civil engineering, was already bored and frustrated with the system. She likes to get things done and in the GDR that was slow and hard work. After the country reunited, with the help of my (other) grandpa, my very supportive dad, a bit of luck and her very own drive she had the opportunity to become General Manager of a road construction company in her late 20ties. For a young woman in the very male-dominated construction industry, this was quite an achievement. While the world around her was disintegrating, she carved out her own path in a chaotic new order, thru cheer determination and about 18+ hours per day in the office for many many years she ended up part owning the business.

This period wasn't just transformative for us—it marked the redefinition of an entire region. Communities were uprooted, identities questioned, and assumptions overturned. The East German experiment ended not with triumph, but with trauma. And yet, it is in that very disintegration that resilience took root. For millions of East Germans, including my family, the fall of the GDR was both an ending and a beginning.

I was very lucky to have grandparents (3 out of 4 still with us as I am writing this book). My dad parents lived by the Baltic Sea and they didn't just look after me during the summer holidays but booked a trip to a different country every year with me and my cousin. My other grandparents still raised my uncle, just over 2 years older than me, a tech genius, introduced me to computers and programming, planting the seeds of a lifelong interest. I still remember watching him debug Turbo Pascal into the early hours of the morning, fascinated how much grief a simple comma can cause. Attention to detail matters!

I was very independent from a young age—I had my own key and walked to and from school from Grade 1. Frequent moves during my early childhood, combined with the fact that everyone around me was so busy, taught me independence and resilience. It also meant I had to solve my own problems. I didn't chase popularity; I valued real, meaningful friendships. I couldn't stay silent when I saw injustice. Even as a child, I had an innate sense of fairness, and I wasn't afraid to speak up for those who couldn't.

Being a teenager during that time was really interesting. Social problems split the youth and therefore my friends, into far left and far right groups. The people around me became more politically polarized, divided between these opposing ideologies. I never liked picking sides because I could understand both points of view, and I had good friends across the whole spectrum.

Despite the tensions, I developed a strong sense of personal security. By age 11, I confidently used public transit alone. I carried a small knife and practiced martial arts, but never truly felt unsafe. After reunification, East Germany's crime rate reached about 10 crimes per 100 people. Still, I found the environment predictable. I wasn't a target and knew how to avoid trouble. I learned early to read my surroundings—to know when to cross the street, be cautious, and navigate crowds. Nothing ever happened to me, nor anyone else close. In additional the awareness proved invaluable in my travels to over 50 countries, including some with high crime rates, where I never faced real danger or lost anything valuable. One of my martial arts teachers was once asked, "What do you do if five people with knives attack you at 3 a.m. in a dark alley?" His answer: "Don't be there." That summed it up for me.

In hindsight, I sometimes wonder if my parents were being a bit irresponsible by letting me navigate the world on my own at such a young age. But now, I'm deeply grateful for that freedom and trust. It's a reminder I carry as a parent myself—how difficult it is to balance protecting our children with allowing them the independence they need to grow strong and self-reliant. In this new world, where safety concerns are always on our minds, finding that balance feels harder than ever. Yet, it's clear to me that nurturing independence alongside care is essential for resilience and confidence.

Looking back, I realise that my parents' greatest gift wasn't just the freedom they allowed me—it was the foundation they laid through their unconditional love and unwavering trust. That, more than structure, more than rules, more than even opportunity, gave me the courage to explore, to take risks, and to believe in myself. It's a life lesson I return to often: when children feel deeply loved and trusted, they learn to trust themselves—and that's the beginning of everything. The world has become a lot less predictable, but that foundation still holds.

Seeds of Global Curiosity and Independence

Eventually, I started working in my mum's company during school holidays. Sometimes I got to ride on a concrete truck, checked invoices, answered the phone as a receptionist, helped prepare and submit tenders, and learned the importance of numbers—not just in school, but in real-world applications. This practical understanding of numbers and productivity proved invaluable for navigating the complex world of logistics, giving me early business experience.

I took every opportunity to travel with my parents, grandparents, uncle, and friends—whether through school programs, holiday trips, or educational excursions—exploring Europe and expanding my view of the world far beyond the grey skies of East Germany. Until I was 10, I had only seen Germany, but by 18, I had visited most countries across the European Union and beyond, including the UK, France, Spain, Croatia, Hungry, Poland, the Czech Republic, Switzerland, Austria, Sweden, Denmark, Turkey, Italy, and Slovakia.

When I was 16, my parents bought their first house, marking a new chapter for our family. At 18, I left home to become an Au Pair in the United States. That was the beginning of everything.

Chapter Two: My Path to Logistics

A Life-Changing Year in the U.S.

At 18, I embarked on a year that profoundly shaped my identity. Living with an American family, I cared for three young children, quickly learned to speak decent English, and discovered the complexities of a nation I had only known through movies and media. For the first time, I encountered racism. Growing up in East Germany, everyone was, German—while there were differences, there wasn't the kind of discrimination I later witnessed, or maybe I was just too naïve to see it. But when my African American friend, who was also a PhD student, was stopped by police every time he crossed from New York City to New Jersey, while I never was, it opened my eyes to realities faced by others.

Living on a tight budget—earning just $139 per week with room and board covered—I learned the true value of financial independence. I worked extra hours whenever I could to fund my travels across the country. I visited iconic places: New York City, Los Angeles, San Diego, the Grand Canyon, Lake Powell, San Francisco, Tucson, Dallas, Cleveland, Philadelphia, Washington, D.C., and Boston. I watched the ball drop in Times Square on New Year's Eve, attended Broadway shows, and marveled at the Statue of Liberty from the Staten Island Ferry—just $2 for the ride!

But my adventures didn't stop there. A pilot friend once let me fly a plane—an exhilarating moment that deepened my sense of freedom and adventure. I went cliff jumping, mountain biking, hiking, enjoyed a limo ride in Las Vegas, and made many wonderful new friends. During my travels, I stayed on a Native American reservation, gaining a unique perspective on history, culture, and the proud nations I had only read about in books.

Each adventure shaped me in ways I couldn't have anticipated. Witnessing the sharp contrasts of American society—immense wealth alongside extreme poverty—made me more aware of the world's complexities and deepened my curiosity about the people and places I visited.

I also experienced kindness I'll never forget. Like the border control officer who let me return from Mexico despite me forgetting half my visa paperwork—I hadn't planned to cross the border and didn't want to lose the papers while backpacking. Young and ignorant, I had no idea how lucky I was. Or the kind owner of a San Francisco hostel who stopped me from spending the night at a bus station. I had budgeted every cent carefully but didn't know about the $20 deposit, so I was initially rejected. I left my backpack at the hostel, spent the day exploring, and planned to sleep at the bus station before my early bus to the airport. But the owner saw me walking and offered me a lift in the hostel's car. I ended up with a home-cooked meal from his girlfriend and a warm, cozy private room.

The lessons I learned during that year of exploration, independence, and growth have stayed with me. More importantly, I believe in the kindness of people—I have experienced it firsthand, so many times.

Leaving the U.S. just days before the events of September 11, 2001 (lucky me again), was a sobering reminder of life's fragility. My pilot friend was about to take off from JFK that morning—he personally knew two of the pilots who lost their lives. I had made many friends in New York City and the surrounding areas, and watching the aftermath unfold from afar was heartbreaking. The experience didn't leave physical scars on me, but it deepened my empathy. It gave me a lasting awareness of how quickly life can change—and a quiet respect for those who live with the aftermath of such trauma.

University Life & Cultural Expansion

That year wasn't just a chapter of self-discovery—it became a foundation for resilience, empathy, and a growing appreciation for the privileges and opportunities I had been given. After my time in the U.S., I returned to Germany to continue my studies, ready to keep expanding my horizons both academically and personally.

My time at university in Osnabrück was especially important. It gave me the chance to meet even more people from all over the world and to grow both in knowledge and in perspective. I enrolled in the International Business and Management program, which brought together about forty students—half German, many with prior life experience, and half international, coming from countries like China, the Philippines, Russia, Belarus, Ukraine, Kazakhstan, India, Spain, Pakistan, Cameroon, Hungary, Brazil, and Venezuela. This rich mix of cultures created an incredible learning environment—both inside and outside the classroom.

We shared meals, stories, and traditions. One of my favourite memories was having Russian-style picnics in the park. We'd buy meat for shashlik, marinate it in wine, beer, or spices, and grill it over charcoal. With music, beer, and great company, we'd talk about life and the world. That's all we needed.

Living with people from such diverse backgrounds also brought small, meaningful cultural lessons. I tasted my first curry thanks to my Pakistani flatmate. Later, my Indian friend's mum introduced me to even more incredible flavours. I learned about traditions and modesty: I once offered my flatmate a spare prayer rug when he asked where to buy one, and I remember the surprise on his cousin's face when he saw me walking around in a towel after a shower (I might have scared him for life). These simple moments of cultural exchange shaped my understanding of what it means to live and work in a globally connected world.

University was about much more than just lectures. I joined AIESEC, a student organisation that gave me opportunities to take on leadership roles, plan events, and collaborate with peers from around the world. Our weekends were full of planning sessions and hard work—it was intense (no sleep!), but incredibly rewarding. AIESEC opened doors for me in ways I didn't expect. Through this network, I first connected with Hellmann Worldwide Logistics. I started with a part-time data entry role in their road division in my first semester, and over time, their global HR manager (who was involved with AIESEC) offered me a project manager position. This was my path into logistics—a field that would shape much of my professional life.

The early 2000s were a fascinating time. The internet was taking off, reshaping communication, commerce, and connection. The dot-com bubble had just burst, and Europe was preparing to adopt the euro in 2002. In our classes and casual discussions, we often talked about China's rapid economic growth, the geopolitical effects of 9/11, and what all these changes meant for our future careers. These weren't abstract ideas—they were the real forces shaping our world.

When I started uni, we didn't have mobile phones yet. In the USA my host parents had a pager. My mum had a mobile phone for work but as a student, this was an unaffordable luxury. As technology rapidly evolved, we kept pace. Social media was slowly emerging and changing how people shared stories and connected. We studied topics like business ethics and technology's role in the workplace. I even chose to focus my master's thesis on business intelligence and knowledge platforms—concepts that were cutting edge at the time but are now part of everyday business strategy.

A World Classroom

My studies didn't just stay within Germany. I took every chance to travel and immerse myself in different cultures. I completed an internship at a bank in Luxembourg—another small but meaningful chapter that broadened my perspective and gave me a glimpse into the world of finance. For my semester abroad I spent six months in Santiago de Cuba, living simply on just $1 a day and learning a third language, I have now mostly forgotten. But the memories remain forever! Even with limited means, life was full of music and movement—salsa dancing at Buena Vista Social Club concerts on campus, and karate lessons thanks to a kind local who gave me a uniform. It was a time of change in Cuba, too. Fidel Castro still gave his daily speeches on television, though just months after I left, he officially stepped down. I loved the warmth—both of the weather and the people.

The constant 32°C heat felt energising to me, though many locals would sigh and complain about it. That's when a deeper truth hit me: I could enjoy the experience precisely because I had the freedom to leave. For me, it was six months of learning and exploration. For them, it was life—with no easy way out.

That contrast stayed with me. It reminded me that a government must do more than rule; it must care for its people, build a strong economy, and most importantly it must protect personal freedoms. Without these foundations, even paradise can feel like a prison.

Stepping Into Logistics

Following the semester abroad, Hellmann offered me to work in Barcelona during my next summer break. I had been thinking about volunteering in Panama, mostly because I didn't want to forget my Spanish—but this seemed like a more sensible career move. I gladly accepted. Since I didn't want my parents financial help, this was a better economic decision too. I absolutely love Barcelona! While there, I took the opportunity to travel through Spain, France, and Andorra, soaking up the diversity of landscapes and cultures. I even made it to Gibraltar and met its famous monkeys. At the time, Spain was still riding a wave of economic growth, and the energy was infectious.

After completing my bachelor's and the first year of my master's, Hellmann sent me to Hong Kong where I ended up working in regional role. The city was vibrant and constantly moving—a mix of East and West still adjusting to its return to China in 1997. I loved it. I tried everything from Brazilian Jiu-Jitsu and Aikido to dragon boating, wakeboarding, hiking, went to islands, beaches, drank way too much, lived on 4 hours of sleep, had the best parties, the list goes on. Despite Hong Kong's nonstop pace, I found peace in early morning runs to the Peak, watching the city wake up. It was an exciting and transformative time in my life. Most importantly I've made some wonderful friends for life.

It was also in Hong Kong that I truly fell in love with logistics. I realised how powerful the industry is—it connects people with products, and people from all cultures with opportunity. With my love of travel and appreciation for multicultural environments, I felt like I was in paradise. Hellmann was incredibly supportive. I was managing the implementation of several clients from both the U.S. and Europe, creating SOPs and training operators on the systems. Over time, I started to notice patterns and realised that 80% of the processes were always the same. When I brought this observation to management, I received full support. With their backing, I rolled out standardised procedures across the Asia region. This initiative became one of the most defining moments of my early career: I was invited to present my work at Hellmann's worldwide meeting in Budapest – representing Asia.

The Heartbeat of Logistics

What stayed with me even more, though, was the universal desire of people to do a good job. Once I documented the standards and offered support through training, I spent significant time with operators across Asia—from India, Bangladesh, Sri Lanka, Vietnam, the Philippines, Indonesia, China, Korea, and beyond. What I discovered was simple yet profound: people just wanted to do the right thing. Given clear direction and the tools to succeed, most were eager and proud to deliver good work.

Of course, I now understand that there are sometimes external pressures or systemic challenges that may cloud this desire. But deep down, I still hold the belief that every employee starts a job with the intention of doing it well—and they thrive when expectations are clear and support is available.

Those early years sealed it for me. I was hooked. I realised that logistics wasn't just a job—it was a passion and a purpose. I was locked in for life, and I've never looked back.

My twenties were filled with questions and discoveries. Travelling, studying, working, and building friendships across cultures gave me a deeper understanding of the world and my place in it. I learned that living your dream isn't about ticking off a checklist of personal milestones. It's about saying yes to new experiences, being open to other perspectives, and finding joy in the small, shared moments—like a meal with friends from different cultures or a sunrise over a bustling city.

These were the years that shaped my outlook. They helped me become more empathetic and grounded. It answered some of my many questions and raised so many more. They also laid the foundation for the work and life that would follow.

Growing Roots in Australia

I met my now-husband while living in Hong Kong, and in 2008, I made the bold decision to move to Australia. It wasn't the most stable time to quit a job, but I packed my life into one suitcase and landed in Melbourne with hope and determination. At just 26, I decided to tone down my CV—transforming "Business Process Manager Asia" into something more in line with a casual working holiday. It worked. Within two days, I landed a job in a call centre.

The real challenge, however, was finding a company willing to sponsor me. Although I could work temporarily on a Work and Holiday visa due to my age, my relationship was still new, and I didn't want to rely on it for residency or support. I had always been proud of carving my own path, and this chapter was no different.

Looking back, arriving in Australia in the midst of the 2008 Global Financial Crisis was a test of both timing and tenacity. The world was reeling from economic shockwaves—major banks were collapsing, stock markets were plummeting, and companies were freezing hiring or downsizing altogether. In Australia, while the impact wasn't as severe as in the U.S. or Europe, businesses were cautious, and job opportunities for newcomers were limited and highly competitive. For a new arrival on a working holiday visa with no local experience, the odds weren't exactly in my favour.

The Unexpected Power of Networking

And yet, sometimes determination carves its own path—and sometimes, that path is shaped by the people who see your potential before you even realise it yourself. This was the first time I truly experienced the power of networking and the strength of genuine friendships. My Aikido instructor from Hong Kong—who also held a senior role at Kuehne + Nagel—reached out to the CEO of KN Australia on my behalf. In his words, I was "tenacious and resilient," lol. That connection led to an interview and eventually a role in Business Development. I always believe in making my own luck. Opportunities often grow from effort, and the quiet confidence others have in you—sometimes before you have it in yourself.

That job was a turning point in my Australian journey. It didn't take long before I was promoted to Key Account Manager, and soon after, K+N sponsored my visa. It wasn't just a job; it was an opportunity. It gave me stability in uncertain times and a clear runway to grow within the logistics industry. The promotion during a time when many companies were hesitant to invest in people felt like both an honour and a validation of the risks I had taken.

While the world was contracting, I was expanding—learning to adapt to a new culture, building a life from scratch, and embedding myself in an industry that would later become central to my professional identity. The GFC taught me that even in times of crisis, opportunity still exists—sometimes disguised—but always there for those willing to work for it. And I learned that relationships—even those formed on the dojo floor—can shape the course of your life. Interestingly, I've since noticed how many people in our industry come from sporting and/or military backgrounds—whether it's AFL, rugby, military or martial arts—bringing with them discipline, teamwork, and resilience. It teaches you to persevere, to adapt quickly, and to stay focused—qualities that are invaluable in logistics and business alike.

After two years at K+N, I moved to Toll Group, where I would spend more than a decade learning the intricacies of international freight, warehousing and domestic transport. Toll was a crash course in scale and complexity. I loved the challenge.

The world outside was changing rapidly, too. The logistics industry and the global landscape were transformed by a series of seismic events. The GFC reshaped economies, and Australia, while resilient, felt the tremors. The rise of China's Belt and Road Initiative, Brexit, the push for digital transformation, and the growing urgency of sustainability became defining themes. Automation, robotics, and data-driven platforms revolutionized the movement of goods. The expansion of the Panama Canal shifted shipping routes, and global trade tensions forced companies to rethink their strategies. By 2020, e-commerce had exploded, and the COVID-19 pandemic thrust supply chains into the spotlight. Suddenly, logistics was no longer invisible; it was essential.

On the personal front, I got married and had the kind of wedding I couldn't have even dreamed of as a child—on a boat, cruising through the incredible city of Melbourne on a hot summer day. While working at Toll, I also became a mum. Between pregnancies, I was promoted. I'll never forget telling the global head of sales at the time that I planned to have more children—his response stuck with me: "That's normal. How else are we going to grow the population? And it certainly shouldn't stop you from receiving a well-deserved promotion."

That moment was one of the reasons I stayed at Toll for so long. I know there are lots of stories, rumours, and challenges associated with the company—I was there through the cyberattacks and plenty of organisational changes—but my personal experience was overwhelmingly positive. I felt supported.

2020 was a watershed year. The pandemic tested every system, both at home and at work. During that time, I was homeschooling three boys while navigating the crazy COVID logistics challenges for many businesses that became clients. I was also involved in Toll's digital transformation projects and managed my team remotely. That year, I achieved my highest sales performance ever—but my real achievement was simply holding it all together, keeping my family safe and my team connected. After that yes, I left there was nowhere else for me to go at Toll. I was on top of the global sales leaderboard and there wasn't another role for me to grow into. The business was consumed with its demerger and internal challenges. It felt like the right time to move on. I remain truly grateful to the people I worked with and the friendships I formed along the way.

I also know the company is in good hands—JP Post and an inspiring, deeply intelligent philanthropist who even took time out of his busy schedule to personally call me when I left. That gesture meant a lot.

Coming from a small family business originally, I spent most of my career up to that point in large corporate companies. I learned how to navigate the systems and politics, but I'll admit, I don't like politics. I like honesty and simple, common sense. Things often moved slowly, decision-making was layered and complex, and I felt boxed in. I felt the glass ceiling or cage.

With my youngest child starting school, it was time to test my own limits—to see how far I could soar. I joined a startup in a related but distinct space: industrial real estate and supply chain consulting. What a journey that was. I also returned to study, balancing work and education over the next few years to refresh and expand my skills in leadership, board governance, and commercial real estate.

Smaller businesses energized me. The ability to implement ideas and witness their immediate impact was deeply rewarding. After the startup, I joined Tasman Logistics and stepped into my most senior role yet. We built new business units, made 2 acquisitions and I helped to grow the business from $80 million to $250 million in turnover. It was also a time when technology moved from being just a concept to something I really needed to understand deeply. I attended conferences and workshops, meeting many smart, passionate people who shared insights about the future of logistics and supply chain. I learned about warehouse automation, smarter scanning and picking systems, real-time tracking, route optimisation, telematics and IoT within the supply chain—tools that are quickly becoming essential for the industry's survival and growth.

One area that particularly caught my attention was alternative fuels. Beyond biodiesel, I learned about a wide range of options being explored globally and here in Australia—from renewable diesel and hydrogen fuel cells to electric trucks and bio-LNG. These fuels offer promising pathways to reduce emissions and help the transport sector transition towards genuine sustainability.

While working closely with the agricultural sector, I uncovered a striking fact: Australia exports tens of thousands of tonnes of tallow (beef fat) overseas each year to be converted into alternative fuels. Considering Australia's massive beef industry—producing around 2 million tonnes of beef annually—it seemed clear that we have a largely untapped domestic resource right at our doorstep. Instead of exporting raw materials, why not build local capacity to turn this into valuable biofuels here?

This isn't just about biodiesel—it applies broadly to many raw materials we export. Yes, labour costs in Australia are higher compared to other countries, but technology and automation have advanced to a point where these challenges can be overcome. With smart investments in automation and innovation, it's possible to build efficient, competitive local production.

I've seen so much box-ticking and short-term thinking across industries, and I'm not a fan of superficial "solutions" that don't deliver real impact. Short government funding cycles often lead to fragmented efforts and uncertainty, which hold back long-term investment and true innovation.

I firmly believe there are real solutions out there—by harnessing our own resources and committing to sustained investment, Australia can lead the way in many sectors. It requires bold vision and significant investment, but the future starts today. Moving beyond surface-level fixes to meaningful, long-term change will build resilience in our economy, create local jobs, and foster sustainable growth. The challenges are complex, but the opportunities are enormous when we commit to real progress.

This journey led me to my current role as General Manager at MCM Logistics. We operate warehouses across six states in Australia and provide transport solutions for anything from a small international parcel to pallets, trucks, containers, and project work. Beyond that, we strive to be trusted advisors to our customers and potential clients. I feel fortunate to be in a position where I can bring together my operational and commercial experience, my passion for growing a business, and my commitment to building a high-performing team—all while staying at the forefront of data-driven insights and the latest technology. I'm hoping to be here for a while and to see just how far our amazing team, MCM, and I can soar together.

Final Reflection

From my 'Ossi' beginnings behind the Iron Curtain to an 'Aussie' life filled with opportunity, I've learned that home isn't just a place—it's where your values, your people, and your purpose come together. I've worked hard, adapted, and kept showing up—and yet, not every part of my journey can be credited to hard work alone. I've been guided, too—by luck, by grace, or by a higher power that nudged me toward the right people, the right moments, and the right choices.

Australia has become home in every sense of the word. I'm surrounded by a loving family and a community of extraordinary people. I've been fortunate to contribute to an industry I care about deeply, and maybe even play a small part in shifting it—toward real solutions, integrity, and innovation.

Along the way, I've learned to say yes to opportunities, even if I wasn't full ready. Because growth often starts with a simple yes. I've also learned that you don't have to walk every path alone. I have my own personal "board of advisors"—friends, mentors, and peers I turn to for wisdom, support, and perspective depending on the challenge.

Most importantly, I've come to understand that you *can* have it all—a family, a career, a sense of purpose—just not always at the same time or in the same way. And that's okay. The balance is fluid, not fixed, and there's great strength in being present for whatever chapter you're in.

I never set out to be a leader or a role model. But I've learned that sometimes leadership looks like listening. Like trying again. Like lifting someone else up, one person at a time.

And in the end, perhaps my belief in fairy tales wasn't so far-fetched after all. Because here I am—a girl born behind an iron curtain, growing roots in a faraway country, surrounded by love and purpose, still dreaming. Not of perfect endings, but of meaningful chapters. And if one day the story feels unfinished or takes an unexpected turn, I'll ask my husband to imagine a better one—just like always.

And then, I'll get back to work on making it real.

Author's BIO
Katharina (Kat) Attana

Katharina (Kat) Attana is a globally experienced supply chain leader, mentor, and advocate for empowered leadership. With over 20 years of success across Europe, the U.S., Asia, and Australia, she currently serves as General Manager at MCM Logistics—a national 3PL and transport solution provider known for innovation and operational excellence.

Kat has held multiple senior executive roles throughout her career, including Chief Commercial Officer at Tasman Logistics, senior leadership at Toll Group and Kuehne + Nagel, and Business Process Manager Asia at Hellmann Worldwide Logistics. Her expertise spans strategic transformation, commercial growth, operational leadership, and building high-performing teams across culturally diverse environments.

Kat is passionate about mentorship and personal growth, actively empowering future leaders in logistics and beyond. As a trusted voice in the industry, she is often invited to speak on leadership, women in logistics, workplace equity, and global supply chain trends. She was honored with the Female Leadership Award by the VTA, a recognition of her trailblazing impact and dedication to shaping a more balanced and inclusive industry.

A proud mother of three boys, Kat holds degrees in International Business, Management, and Commercial Real Estate, and is a graduate of the Australian Institute of Company Directors. Through her leadership, mentoring, and speaking, Kat is committed to helping professionals unlock their potential and thrive with purpose, confidence, and courage.

LinkedIn: https://www.linkedin.com/in/katharina-zink-attana-b479b2/

Chapter 6

The Long Haul
Building a Legacy Through Purpose, People, and Perseverance

How a Freight Leader Navigated Crisis, Connection, and Change to Build a Business That Lasts

Gavin Homer

Chapter One: Choices, Challenges & Cargo: My Journey Through the Skies and Supply Chains

Thrown Staplers and Tough Starts: Baptism by Fire in Freight

Back in the early Nineties an old boss of mine screamed a tirade of personal obscenities at me, final statement being "you won't get anywhere in life!" Not unusual for him or of management style back then. This was a crazy day, where a few hours earlier my then supervisor had argued with this boss, resulting in the boss throwing a stapler at him, narrowly missing thankfully. Not surprisingly the supervisor had run out of the office, straight down to a local staff agency to find another job!

I'd missed all the action as I'd been collecting documents from the airlines at Birmingham Airport and walked right into the middle of this drama. The boss called me in to his office, shouted the obscenities at me and told me to learn exports, take the supervisor challenge or get the hell out of the place.

Not much of a choice really as I wanted to pursue a career in logistics so I took the decision to learn exports, stay and prove to him I could get "somewhere in life". I rose to the challenge of being the supervisor, obviously hopeful he would not throw a stapler at me one day too!

This was in 1991 when the world was a very different place, with no mobile phones, no social media and certainly not much care for human resources in business. I'd started in the industry back in 1988 working for what was then one of the United Kingdom's largest freight companies, Meadows Freight.

I did better than expected at school, went to a local Sixth Form College in Solihull, where I grew up and stumbled into freight. I've always been passionate about travel, mad about aircraft, and an avid aviation enthusiast. I studied History and Geography at "A" Level, so I knew I wanted to do something around travel.

Back then travel agencies were huge, so I'd done a little work experience with a tour operator at college, considered travel agencies, air traffic controller but being colour blind that was a non-starter. I wasn't even sure I wanted an office job, so I considered careers such as the forestry commission or working for the National Trust. It was at a career's day where the local manager of Meadows Freight was exhibiting, he said "have you thought about Freight Forwarding". It wasn't Logistics back then; it was freight which I knew nothing about but was hooked when he said it involved working near the local airport dealing with Customs.

After a brief spell in insurance which I hated, my older brother did that for a living, I got offered a chance to join Meadows, starting on the import department to learn Customs declarations. The knowledge that the guys taught me back then me was incredible, one of them being nicknamed "the walking tariff" as he knew every HS code more or less by heart. Before computers, everything was manual, and it would take days to classify one huge import declaration, but it was fascinating. For me it was a great opportunity, oddly I was by far the youngest in the department but the only person who could drive.

A big part of my job was taking a little van; they owned down to the airport to collect the import documents from the airlines. I'd go back later with Customs declarations to present to HMRC and so my days continued. A little bit of doing the paperwork and going down to the airport where I got to see the planes!

Whilst Meadows was one of the largest freight companies in the United Kingdom it got bought out not long after I joined, became Walford Meadows and then very quickly after that bought again to become Rockwood. From my recollection Rockwood was more of an investment group who stripped the assets of companies and sold them on. At the time I didn't know this but soon people were being made redundant, offices closed, and the business slowly collapsed. As I lived at home with mom and dad, I stayed throughout most of that period, still learning imports and still driving what became a little Rockwood van around the airport.

The industry was very badly paid back then, not that well recognized and most people didn't even know what a freight company did. I guess some of that continues today as anyone not involved in logistics tends to think goods magically arrive without all that goes on behind the scenes.

Most of my friends had gone into IT, paid about four or five times what I took home, but that seemed very boring to me, you'd sit all day in front of one of those new 'computer things' writing programs. Still to this day IT frustrates the hell out of me, if it doesn't work straight away, I want to throw it out of the window. So glad I did not pursue a career in technology!

Looking back on the start of my journey life is always about choices. The choice I made in the early days to go into freight, something I knew little about back then, would become a lifelong passion. After the Rockwood fiasco came my next choice, one of my worst ever as a shipping line head hunted me, and I went to work for them thinking it would be glamourous. I absolutely hated my short period working there. One of the worst bosses I recall, who just sat there all day reading the newspaper, shouting orders and calling me "boy". Again, I was the youngest in the department, the only one who could drive, and I ended up becoming the bosses taxi service.

Whilst the liner was the wrong choice for me as I did not fit that culture, in the eighteen months I was there I learnt a huge amount, met a really good friend who we'll talk about later and realised working for a logistics company was what I needed to do. Plus, I missed the planes, so what on earth possessed me back then to go and work with a shipping line who knows.

That choice was not a great one, but it helped build my character as some of my colleagues were hard to deal with and I had to face that challenge. I've always been quiet, unassuming, certainly very honest in my beliefs and it was quite a shock to be part of a culture where people would stab each other in the back to get a promotion. Little did I know what lay ahead, but that was certainly a grounding in corporate life.

The Garden Shed Years: Leadership, Loyalty, and Loss

Back to 1991 and my stapler throwing boss. After the liner I'd joined this German logistics conglomerate, who later got taken over by the Scandinavians and are now growing to be one of the largest logistics providers in the world. Their Birmingham Office was a strange place, a large garden like shed in the middle of the staff car park at the airport. It was a great place to work, even nearer the planes. In the summer it was like a hothouse, so you'd have the doors open, in the winter it was like a fridge, but it was a fantastic atmosphere.

Accepting the challenge to step up to supervisor and learn exports was the right choice, even under trying circumstances. It meant I started to get more involved in customer service and joined our salesman on sales calls. I learnt so much from him, one of the industries greatest salesmen in my opinion. Honesty and integrity were his style, not just winning the client but offering them a solution that worked for them.

In those early days I started to realise my passion was always to help the customer, not just about the company profit margin. A real challenge when you work for a large multi-National with targets to achieve but if you are true to your heart and clients believe in you, I am a firm believer that they'll put their trust in you. Back then I recognized that I thrived on the challenges of problem solving, finding bespoke solutions for business to move their goods and I just loved the industry.

With the supervisor role came taking responsibility for a team of people. Most of my team were very young and I really enjoyed encouraging them so they could thrive. Like many new leaders I know I made some mistakes around people management, but I learnt from those and found real satisfaction in seeing the team get on and grow together.

I'd always thought being the interviewee was hard, you go to an interview, you've planned for what you want to say, read up on the company you want to join and it's so important to get that job. However, from an early start in management I felt being the interviewer was just as hard too. How do you decide if someone is going to fit your team, do a good job for the business and hopefully stay the term in just a few hours. Yes, you can conduct tests, set challenges or just chat to the prospective employee but you only get to find out who they are once they're on board. From those early days I always thought you should pick someone with passion, drive and energy; the business you can teach. That's why I've always been so keen to employee young people and help teach them the logistics industry. You obviously need experience in your team I don't deny, but the chance to see someone new grow with you is just so rewarding.

So, my recruitment days started, and we built a great team around us and operated successfully out of the garden shed. One eventful night the stapler throwing boss had a heart-attack in the minibus back from the company Christmas party in London.

One of my best friends, longest friends who I still enjoy some crazy nights out with today saved his life on that bus. He was our air export guru, he taught me exports, but he was also really keen on his Health & Safety. He knew what to do when the boss had a heart-attack, and on the side of the road saved his life. This led to several months of the boss being in hospital, me and the team running the office and everything thrived. However, for me it was probably then I realised putting your trust in people has it's risks. The business did not feel I was the right man to head up the branch, so one of the Directors chose to send a guy from London up to manage the team. He did nothing except take people out for lunch, a few drinks, talk the talk and I soon realised he took all the credit for the success of Birmingham.

I'd always liked to be in the shadows, I didn't want the limelight, so I just let this happen. Then while the boss was in hospital, the guy from London was getting all the accolades, my family had a huge shock, my mom passed away suddenly from a heart attack.

I'd had a great family life, born in the late sixties to older parents and older siblings around me. My sister is very musical and studied at music college, my brother worked in insurance at the time. We were a really close family, held together by my mum but we had some fantastic times. My brother introduced me to planes, so I was lucky from an early age to travel the world with him photographing aircraft. The shock of losing mom was hard, she'd always been there to support us all. I moved out of home, bought my first place near the airport and started to fight for my career. I knew by then this was the work path for me.

The boss recovered from his heart attack but never did return to work, we got a new boss, who apart from the fact he could "talk for England" was a great inspiration. He'd call you to a meeting, repeat the same story over and over again to the point we had an agreement in the team, a staff member would make an excuse someone was on the phone, so they'd knock on the door and get you out. However, he supported me, and the business moved out of the garden shed into a fancy new logistics centre just north of Birmingham.

Family had been a huge part of my life, we did so much together so the initial living alone was a challenge as we were very close and remain that way today. I'd always wanted to meet someone but that had not happened, so I moved out of home to live alone, by some miracle managed to get the bank to support a mortgage on my lousy salary and bought my first place. It was quite an adventure and around this time I made friends with a great group of people all around the same age at work. I grew to survive alone and even managed to get a raise out of the boss which meant I was only broke half the time. Looking back, I now know these early days of hard work and determination set a path for my future, perhaps unwittingly.

From Quiet Determination to Building Something Bold

It was around this time I started looking for promotion opportunities and volunteered to be involved with British Standards (now ISO) to get more exposure in the wider business. I stayed there, learnt so much but by the Millenium I realised they were never going to promote me, so to have the chance of furthering my career I had to take a gamble. That gamble was with the friend from the liner I mentioned earlier. We started a Birmingham office from the ground up for a UK-based project cargo forwarder. It was just a fantastic experience, such exciting times, scary too but what an opportunity for the quiet kid from Solihull.

So, in January 2000 we opened the office, just two of us for a project forwarder. That took me out of the comfort zone of working for a huge multinational company to the world of the SME where every job, sale, piece of freight really matters. We were lucky as we got off to a great start but soon it became apparent, I had to get out and sell. This was scary at first as I didn't have that great sales guy to accompany me on sales calls, it was me in my car driving thousands of miles around the country, alone, but building connections.

For all of those involved in sales everyone knows it's a mix of highs and lows, some great days when you make a phone call and they say yes, bad days when you drive to the other side of the country to no luck. I was always honest, did not try and sell a service we could not do, but I really liked the challenge of meeting, and hopefully exceeding the demands of a client.

My nature might be one of a quiet person, but I have always liked pushing myself and enjoyed meeting people from different backgrounds. Out on the road selling in logistics is so rewarding because you learn so much about myriads of different businesses. I'd encourage anyone new to the industry to listen to their clients, learn about their businesses, their families and what their passion is for success. This way you get to understand so much more about your clients' needs so you can offer them something special, a solution perhaps no other provider has yet offered. Whilst the logistics industry is very price driven, often there are costs savings in the solutions you can provide a business rather than pursuing the race to the lowest possible freight rate.

Trust, Betrayal, and the Heathrow Fightback

During the early 2000's was a great time for prosperity and our new venture grew in Birmingham quite nicely. However, the company I worked for had an office based at Heathrow Airport. Being someone from an airfreight background I had helped on occasions when they were short-staffed. One day in early 2001, working down at the Heathrow office I noticed much of the work they were doing was being released to another company. Very strange, this company also had the initials of the then boss and an ex-staff member who had now left and gone to work there! A little bit of easy "Sherlock Holmes" detective work and I put two and two together and realised they were in cahoots to take all the business.

So, I rang the Directors who immediately came from head office to Heathrow, confronted the boss who admitted his plan and was relieved of his duties. The Directors asked me to be interim Manager of the branch and help fight to keep the business.

Consequently, there was yet another choice. I had agreed to build a Birmingham office with a friend of mine and was now being asked to help save a Heathrow office too. Looking back, perhaps my friend was not too happy about this as it left him with sole pressure for Birmingham, but we agreed I had to do this and put the effort into helping the business save Heathrow. Hence, that's what I did, and I was even nearer the planes at Heathrow, which I loved and had always spent countless hours for my hobby being there too.

An odd thing happened; the guy who'd taken all the accolades to save the Birmingham Branch at my previous employer had become a good friend of mine. He lived just by Heathrow airport and offered to put me up Monday to Friday while I was fighting to save the Heathrow branch. So, I began a period of working five days a week in Heathrow, going home to my flat in Birmingham for the weekends.

The challenge of saving this branch was so exciting but at the same time daunting as the previous management had no doubt planned this for many months if not years. They had put in place people and a structure which, had

I not been there, would have allowed them to take all that branch of business to their new start up. Very devious and conniving but that gave me the drive to make sure they did not win. I put my heart and soul into saving the branch, employed some good friends of mine who would support me and we turned it around. Yes, they took some business, but we kept a huge part and by driving countless hours around the UK knocking on doors I built some new business too. It was a fantastic time in my life and looking back subconsciously set my desire to run my own company.

You've probably gathered by now that the story I want to share is one that life is full of choices. Often you make the right ones, often you make the wrong ones and sometimes they are presented to you in a way where there is little choice. I knew by now I wanted to be successful in the industry but always felt management wherever I worked did not really believe in my abilities.

Now we go back to the 'friend' who had taken all the accolades to save Birmingham who I was staying with in London. He approached me in 2003 and said an Australian forwarder we both knew wanted to open in the UK. He would be Managing Director based at Heathrow, I could be General Manager based in Birmingham, open my own office and get my own team. What a strange turn of events, of all the people to step up and believe I could do something like this, but it was an opportunity I could not turn down, no choice here. With it came the chance of more money, a better company car and the chance to do business travel and build on the worldwide contacts I had started to nurture.

The story so far has been mostly about my career. I had grown up in a very ordinary family, stumbled into this career in logistics, lost my mother at a fairly young age and followed a passion for aviation. I'd always wanted to meet someone; I was down at a local pub in Solihull back in 1999 when I met my now wife Reka. She is from Hungary, and I think one of the first people I ever met who believed in me, pushed me and wanted me to succeed regardless of the challenges that face me. She had moved in with me by now so whilst I had been going back and forth to Heathrow she had been here in Birmingham. We had considered moving to Heathrow together, but when the opportunity came along to open my own branch in Birmingham it meant I could be back with Reka full-time. Reka was so supportive of this next choice that it made it easy to make the move.

So, in 2003, I resigned my position as interim Heathrow manager and took the role as General Manager for a UK start-up owned by our Australian parent company. The worldwide economy was thriving, the business to Australia boomed both sea and air so we got off to a great start. I had the opportunity to do lots of business travel, meetings in Australia, China, Hong Kong, as well as visiting agents in the USA; it was just incredibly exciting.

Reka and I got married in July 2005, one of the best days of my life. We had moved into a new house back in 2004, had a little more money and the choices made started to reap rewards.

Then in 2006 whilst I was on an overseas trip to South Africa, Reka called me, I was in a hotel bar with a colleague. It had been an interesting trip, South Africa is a wonderful place, but full of challenges. Business wise it was great, but on that night, it just got even better. Reka called me and told me she was pregnant. The most exciting news ever, I tried to hide it from my colleague but there was just no way, it was obvious, and they realised what I'd been told straight away!

Something I had always dreamt about, and better still we found out later we were expecting a daughter. In 2006 Stephanie (Stephie) was born, 7 weeks prematurely, but thanks to a fantastic neonatal unit she has done so well, turned 19 this year and started a great university close to us. For Reka and I, Stephie is the best thing we have ever done.

Being a dad is without a doubt the best role ever and playing a part in bringing Stephie up has been crucial to me. I've been very lucky that whilst I had a demanding job, I always managed to take Stephie to school, perhaps one of the oldest dads at the school gate but being there for her has always been our number one priority. You can make many choices in life but one thing I would say is however many demands work puts on you find time for the family. "Work life balance" is everything a good friend always says to me.

With a career going well, a new baby, my wife and I were delighted with where we were in life. We made another choice that Reka would not go back to work, we would manage on one income so that she could devote her time to bringing up Stephie, allowing me the chance to concentrate on building the business. It was hard sometimes, long days, overseas travel, missing the family but the passion for logistics remained. With full support of Reka I pushed on to help grow the UK branches to a 16 million turnover company by 2009.

During this time, I employed some great young people, straight from school on "training courses" that would now be called apprenticeships. Seeing young people start in the industry, helping to train them and nurture them as I mentioned before has always been a passion of mine. We had a great team in both London and Birmingham which was the backbone of the success of the company. However, in 2009 my friend, the Managing Director, rang me one day and said he'd just taken a call from the CEO in Melbourne. They had decided to sell the UK business to some friends who owned a freight company in Staines, and strangely the guys involved in that business also owned a chain of Italian restaurants!

In hindsight my friend and I made the wrong choice when starting the business as we did it all as employees rather than asking for shares in the business. Perhaps we would never have been offered the opportunity had we asked, we will never know. Yes, we'd been well paid, but we made huge profits for the Australian owners, and they sold the business to friends. Nothing we could do about it, their business and their prerogative, but one thing I knew from that moment was that I could no longer stay. It was one of the easiest choices I had ever made in my career, I knew I had to leave but what would I do. The last 6 years had given me so much experience in running a business, selling, and building connections that I felt it was time to start my own company.

A New Legacy: Founding Atlas Logistics UK

Life is all about connections too, and all those years back working for the Scandinavian company, assisting on sales I'd been involved with Atlas Logistics PVT in India ("Atlas"). I'd built a rapport with the team in India and logistics solutions to/from India had been a huge part of my working life to that date. In 2004 the Scandinavian company had bought an Indian business and effectively fired Atlas as their partners. The Chairman, reached out to me whilst working for the Australians and asked us to represent them in the UK.

We had been doing that successfully since 2004, building import and export consolidations to from India. A tough market as anyone reading will know, difficult to make money due to competition but where there is a will there is a way. The Atlas India chairman always said he wanted a UK business so when the Australians sold, I picked up the phone and asked him if we could start. He said he'd been waiting for the call for years, and what seemed like the following day he flew to London and the bones of Atlas Logistics UK Ltd began to emerge.

Initially it was a joint venture between me, the friend I set up the Birmingham branch for the projector forwarder, a good client of mine and Atlas India. 25% each was how it was planned, and all parties had to stump up capital. The only way I could stump up mine was with personal guarantees, thankfully Reka was in full support. If memory serves me right, I believe she said something along the lines of "just do it, then you can't complain about the boss!"

So, in 2009, the time of a worldwide financial crisis we met in Hong Kong and agreed to start the business. Next came telling the Australian owners I wasn't staying, that was a surreal experience. They turned up in Birmingham thinking I would stay, I handed them my notice and told them what I planned to do with Atlas, the new office being across the corridor!

Like many people in this position, they offered me a great deal to stay but it was too late. I knew I must do this next venture for myself and not have the risk of someone taking all the achievements away from me. So began a six month notice period, which they held me to for the last minute on the final day. They employed a new manager for Birmingham who was a nice guy and to my delight one of my colleagues wanted to follow me to the new venture. Atlas began across the corridor with my friend, an ex-employee and the joint venture partnership with India.

The first six months were challenging as I could not be part of the business, but it got off the ground well thanks to great support. The team grew and once I was able to join fully, we opened a Heathrow Office for airfreight, something critical for business growth. For personal reasons my friend decided the venture was not for him and the owner of the UK business that invested in us also decided to exit. Very early on I had to find the money to buy these two parties out and it became me and Atlas India building the business together, I was back out on the road travelling the globe to push the Atlas name. There is nothing more rewarding than nurturing a business from the start, but at the same time hard work, especially around the time of the credit crunch.

Thanks to my wife and the support of the team we were able to grow Atlas and most days I was still able to take my daughter to school. It was not easy and meant slow and steady growth of the business because the global market was in tough times.

Chapter Two: Choices That Define Us – The Atlas Journey

Foundations Built on Client-Centric Solutions

Initially the company had started with a focus on air export to India, having IATA membership from day one, we moved some good volumes weekly by air from Heathrow to Bangalore and Mumbai. We were also growing our import solutions, air and ocean from Asia and the Indian sub-Continent. We invested money in Customs links to the major ports and airports around the UK, so beginning our focus on customs brokerage and import solutions. To set the business aside from the competition it was crucial to provide bespoke solutions for our clients that meet their needs, not building a business where the client had to meet our requirements. That ethos continues in the business today and we are very proud of offering client bespoke solutions.

Independence, Rebranding, and a New Vision

Moving forward to 2011 Atlas Logistics PVT in India was sold to the SBS Group in Japan and our Chairman looked to retire. We moved to larger premises in both Birmingham and Heathrow, the team grew, and so too the business at a steady pace.

In late 2015 through consultation with the group I agreed to buy the UK company in its entirety, so Atlas Logistics UK Ltd became a totally separate entity to that of the Indian, Japanese group. This was hugely challenging both personally and for the business, but so exciting as it was like a rebirth of Atlas. It was one of those times when it never felt to me that there was a choice, we have a great business, a fantastic team, a loyal customer base who without them there is no business. So began our next phase of ownership by me and a new focus on building the brand. Throughout 2016 we invested in the brand, new logo, new image that remains with us today and clearly differentiates us from our past Indian connections. We worked on a new website, and we decided to really promote what we are good at, going the extra mile and putting the customer first.

Warehousing, Brexit, and Resilience Through Change

With this new focus came the desire to be recognized so we successfully gained accreditation in both ISO9001 and ISO27001; and in 2018 went a step further and gained AEO(F) accreditation with HMRC. Throughout this period, we had been growing our import product and developing consolidation solutions by sea from Asia. In May 2019 we decided to take the plunge and get into warehousing, as luck would have it our landlord in Birmingham had space on site, so we opened a HMRC ETSF facility. We began unpacking containers ourselves, making FBA deliveries nationwide and really growing our import solutions. This developed into offering a pick, pack solution, general warehousing and eCommerce final mile solutions.

Today our Birmingham facility is more than 50,000sqft over two sites and warehousing has become a huge part of what we do. That choice to bring as much as we can inhouse, handle our own warehousing, Customs, be accredited for what we do has been a significant part of our growth.

Throughout this journey people have always been a key part of business success and we are delighted so many of the team have remained at Atlas since the start. We have also employed many young people who have been part of the journey, some have moved on but many are still a key part of the business. Seeing people grow both personally and within the business gives me a great feeling of achievement. I'd like to think because we look after our team that is why they give so much back. That ethos of customer service remains and will always be the most important part of the service we give in my opinion. I have always cared about our clients and wanted to see them succeed, go the extra mile so they can, and our team believe in that too.

On a recent sales day a fellow Logistics Legend @Mandy Deakin-Snell, who in her previous role was a customer of ours. Mandy mentioned that what sets us apart is our focus on going the extra mile; we were her go to logistics provider if you need help in a crisis. What an accolade that is and it makes me feel the choices made on this journey have stood the test of time and proved we're on the right track.

Running a business is not easy, every day there are challenges and rising to those is what sets us all apart. In the UK logistics industry, there was no bigger challenge than the BREXIT years. What a time for our industry and one that most of us look back on and ask the question "how did we do it?". So many hurdles to overcome around new customs systems, new legislation, millions of additional customs declarations, new software, new hardware and countless sleepless nights at the start to ensure goods moved smoothly whilst the myriads of changes went on in the background. I'm proud to say both personally and business wise we survived, we thrived, and goods do still move between the EU and UK. For some sectors, such as excise, food and plants, it has been hard, but we're still there building bespoke solutions in challenging areas of the logistics sector. The extra costs have had an impact on pricing for many goods, but the industry has stepped up to the challenge, kept the goods we all need moving and I'm delighted that Atlas has been able to play a part in this. With our customs brokerage experience we began offering solutions for many businesses, and our ETSF in Birmingham became a critical part of our unique solutions.

It only goes to show the choices made to invest in doing our own customs, being in warehousing, having ETSF facilities paid off in the long run and helped Atlas offer solutions that help and continue to support our clients today. For me, sometimes you can make business choices at the time not knowing if there will be an immediate benefit but just knowing it should be done to offer that solution to your clients.

eCommerce, Expansion, and Going Global

The investment is often a gamble but, in many cases, can prove to have its rewards down the line. Another example of this is the ever-growing eCommerce market globally which exploded during the COVID pandemic. That was another challenging time for every industry, none more than logistics, where I think most of us went into it thinking the worst. However, looking back who would have known consumers would switch to buying so much online which has seen a growth in eCommerce that I personally doubt will ever happen again. Pretty much straight off the back of BREXIT the industry had to meet the challenges of COVID, the sudden need for people to work at home in a culture where most logistics providers never did home working as being in the office 24/7 was seen as a must to both get the job done and impress management! We embraced the home working, invested in the hardware to facilitate this and still adopt a hybrid solution today, except the warehouse, as you can't really unload trucks, containers or operate a fork-lift from home.

The growth in eCommerce was another choice for me, do we be a part of this, in a small way or not? The answer was obviously yes as we already had FBA experience, our warehouse, our ETSF, so the next step of offering pick, pack and final mile was obvious. Today our warehouse looks after many different clients offering B2B and B2C solutions linked to our import functions so setting us apart from those who outsource much of this work to third parties they cannot control. Bringing us right up to date to 2024 we also opened a Manchester office which is a joint venture with one of our eCommerce warehouse partners.

Having never really marketed Atlas at home or on the global stage, the growth has been very much word of mouth, we recently started a marketing campaign. Our management team have been attending networking events globally, we're more visible at both international and local conferences pushing our brand and shouting about what we do. We're building strong alliances with software partners integral to the growth of our business, making those choices that put us right at the forefront of innovation in the industry too. These connections should hold us strong for the future, always adapting to change and ready to take the next step.

Reflections, Relationships, and the Road Ahead

The reason for telling the story of the Atlas journey which can be seen on our website https://atlaslogistics.co.uk/company-timeline/ is success can take many paths and doesn't have to be rushed. With the team I celebrated the business being 15 years old in 2024. Perhaps we could have built the business quicker, but this journey I believe defines what I am, what I hope Atlas is and above all what I feel our customs, suppliers and staff expect from the team. Hard work, dedication and the desire for the long haul reap rewards.

It's difficult in the world today to be a thoughtful leader and often it has given me huge heartache but from those early days when I realised being part of the competitive corporate world was not for me, to today encouraging so many people from different backgrounds to come together and succeed has been and always will remain inspirational.

Logistics as a career for me has been eye opening. It is so fascinating all the different business and characters you get to meet. I know that it has always driven my passion as one minute you can be talking to a eCommerce importer, the next plants from Europe, or a supplies exporter, or a car parts importer or an upcoming retail brand; you name it in logistics most of us have probably move if from A to B.

Life is full of choices, but one of the best choices you can make is supporting others and seeing them grow. I'm so proud of my daughter's success in getting to the university of her choice, and proud to see employees past and present who have gone on to make the logistics industry their chosen career. Recently I was at an awards ceremony which celebrates both industry successes but that of individuals too. The characters who make the industry great, the next generation joining who will take it forward with new ideas, the green revolution, better training, better human resources and hopefully better recognition for the industry will make it a great career for those involved.

Along with choices, a big part of this story was about the connections I've made throughout the journey. Going back to before I started in logistics, that job in insurance I hated, the boss there said, "never fall out with people on the way up in case you need them on the way back down". It's always held with me to never fall out with people, however challenging that may be. I know there have been times when there has been no choice but to do so, and I'm sure others felt the same about me. However, building strong connections, retaining relationships through good and bad, has not only made me stronger, but built my character and I believe made Atlas stronger today. To make a business work you need to engage with and work with so many different people and it's so great when you catch up years later and end up working together on the next exciting project.

Recently I have joined some advisory groups and started much more global networking. It's fascinating swapping stories, ideas and being part of hopefully educating the next generation. Catching up with old friends along the way. You spend so much time working in your life you must enjoy what you do in my opinion, and you must have challenges to make you rise and reach the next goal that you may have felt unattainable before you went for it.

Being a listener is also a huge part of our industry, learning constantly, listening to the needs of your clients and being aware of changing regulations around the world. Therefore you remain agile and ready to deal with that next challenge, because you are already part-way prepared in your own mind before it happens.

Telling my career story, that has spanned almost 40 years, has been hugely invigorating for me and I really hope it inspires others to push on and make their lives, their careers in logistics as rewarding as I feel mine has been. It's challenging but never boring, global trade is constantly impacted by what happens in the world around us. There's never a dull moment and such huge opportunities to push yourself outside your comfort zone.

My career has always will be a huge part of me, I remain the kid who watched planes, fascinated by how they work, inspired by how we move goods around the globe who fell into a career in logistics. I'm eternally grateful I made that choice and can't wait to see what happens next. Choices, good or bad, make them, stand by them, own them and reap the rewards, so when you look back you realise what the journey has taught you.

Here's to decision making, whether wrong or right; take them!

Author's BIO
Gavin Homer

Founder & CEO, Atlas Logistics UK Ltd
Mentor | Logistics Strategist | Thought Leader in
Global Supply Chains

Gavin Homer is the Founder and CEO of **Atlas Logistics UK Ltd**, a high-performing logistics firm headquartered in the UK. With nearly 40 years of experience in the industry, Gavin is a recognized leader who has navigated some of the sector's most complex challenges—from BREXIT to the eCommerce boom—while steering Atlas to sustained, innovation-driven growth.

Since founding Atlas in 2009, Gavin has transformed the company into a trusted logistics provider with a bespoke, customer-first ethos. Under his leadership, Atlas has earned **ISO 9001:2015**, **ISO 27001:2022**, and **AEO(F)** accreditations, expanded its warehousing capacity to over 50,000 sq. ft., and launched innovative customs brokerage and eCommerce solutions trusted across the UK and beyond.

A **Fellow of the Institute of Freight Professionals** and **Member of the Chartered Institute of Logistics and Transport**, Gavin is also part of the **ATeM global advisory group**, where he contributes strategic insights and mentorship to emerging logistics leaders worldwide.

Known for empowering the next generation, Gavin has made it a priority to train, uplift, and retain young professionals, creating an inclusive company culture that celebrates growth from within. His people-first leadership philosophy has earned Atlas a loyal team and customer base—and has cemented his reputation as a mentor and values-based entrepreneur.

Beyond logistics, Gavin is a passionate aviation enthusiast, a curious world traveler, and a lifelong music lover who shares his interests with his daughter. He lives in **Solihull, UK**, with his wife Reka and daughter Stephanie.

◆ **Looking Ahead**

Gavin is open to sharing his experience through **advisory roles, keynote speaking, mentorship, or podcast interviews**, especially in areas of supply chain transformation, entrepreneurship, and industry leadership. His goal? To inspire and enable more people to build resilient businesses rooted in purpose, people, and long-term vision.

Linkedin: https://www.linkedin.com/in/gavin-homer-0b1b5b42/

Chapter 7
The Power Within
Stories of Transformation and Triumph

Monica Arce

Chapter One: The Dream That Was Born When My Daughters Were Nine

From Survival to Self-Discovery
I got married at 21. It was what was expected: to start a young family, as dictated by the culture and customs of Guadalajara in the 1970s. Very soon, my twin daughters arrived, and with them, the apparent "complete package" of happiness: marriage, healthy children, a nice house, and even a family car. However, something inside me wasn't right. I felt empty, lifeless. My immaturity didn't allow me to understand why, but I knew it: I wasn't happy.

I lived trapped in a marriage with a narcissistic man who controlled all my decisions. I was completely dependent: emotionally, economically, and mentally. My dreams... simply didn't exist. I was in a state of pure survival.

Until one day, a teacher came into my life and spoke to me about awareness, about looking within. And then it all began. It was as if someone had lit a spark that had been dormant. I began to read, to study, to open my mind to new ideas.

Breaking Free: The First Step Toward Independence
I was fascinated by everything: finance, science, spirituality, philosophy. In books, I found a universe of possibilities. And finally, my own dreams began to emerge.

I want to learn languages, do sports, study, and grow. But when I brought it up with my husband, his answer was always the same: "That's not possible." After months of internal struggle, one night I saw myself projected forty years into the future, living a life that wasn't mine. I felt terrified. That's when I knew what I had to do.

I decided to get divorced.

Rewriting My Future: From Fear to Action
Starting from scratch wasn't easy. I was only 25 years old, and my daughters were just eight months old. It was like throwing myself into the ocean without knowing how to swim. Anxiety and fear paralyzed me, but something stronger pushed me to make that decision: the need to become an independent woman and be able to support my family without relying on anyone.

Ten months after the separation, I decided to look for my first job. My daughters were already a year and a half old. I needed a job that would allow me to spend as much time as possible with them. Looking for a job without experience and without knowing what position to apply for caused me a lot of uncertainty. The only thing I had was that I needed to at least cover my basic monthly expenses.

Every day I would check the local newspapers where companies posted job openings. I sent my resume to various companies. I received responses from most of them, and I attended all the interviews. I kept doing this for three months. Even though they were willing to hire me, I always found an excuse not to accept. Fear paralyzed me; it kept me from moving forward.

During those three months of interviews, I fought an internal battle I didn't know how to name it. Every time they called to confirm I had been selected, my mind went into panic. I had a conversation inside of me, with things like: "You're not going to make it," "What if you fail?" "What if your daughters need you and you're not there?" "There must be someone better than you."

I dressed in a professional dress code for my first interviews with my heart racing, practiced my answers in front of the mirror, and tried to appear confident. But as soon as I walked out with a job offer, the voice of self-sabotage would show up, disguised as logic: "That job is too far," "The schedule isn't ideal," "Maybe the salary doesn't justify the sacrifice."

And although some of those excuses seemed reasonable, deep down I knew it wasn't the schedule, or the traffic, or the salary: it was fear. A fear that came from way back, from years of feeling incapable, invisible, silenced.

In silence, I felt ashamed of myself. How could I want to move forward if I didn't even dare to begin?

There was one interview in particular I will never forget. The company was small, the position was ideal, the environment felt welcoming. Everything seemed aligned. I walked out smiling, and when they called to offer me the job, I declined without hesitation. I hung up the phone and burst into tears. That time I couldn't lie to myself anymore: I was my biggest obstacle.

That night, I sat in the kitchen with a notebook. I wrote down everything I was afraid of. A long, raw, painful list. Then, on the next page, I wrote what I wanted to achieve. Seeing it so clearly helped me realize something important: my dreams were bigger than my fears.

I decided to stop waiting to "feel ready" and just take the first step. I promised myself I would accept the next offer. Even if I trembled. Even if I didn't know how. Even if I cried on the first day.

And so it was. The next opportunity came. And this time, I said yes.

I accepted my first job although the salary was minimum wage. I was hired as the assistant to the director of a small company. The general director was a friend of the family, and I felt a sense of obligation. I didn't know much about office work or reports, but I had something that didn't appear on a resume: an absolute determination to move forward.

I was to start the very next day. Fortunately, we already had a nanny, Vicky, who would take care of my daughters while I was away.

One of the biggest challenges was that, for the first time, I would be separated from my daughters. When I said goodbye, they clung to my skirt crying. I cried as I got into the car. I had to be strong; I was carrying an enormous responsibility on my shoulders.

That drive to the office was one of the longest of my life, even though it lasted just fifteen minutes. I had a knot in my stomach, a mix of guilt, fear, and uncertainty. I asked myself if I was doing the right thing, if my daughters would be okay, if I would be able to adapt to that new environment... or if I would turn around and run as soon as I stepped inside.

I entered the building trembling inside, but with the best smile I could fake. They gave me a simple desk, an old computer, and a pile of documents I didn't fully understand. Everything was new: the terms, the systems, the dynamics. Even the way coworkers spoke to each other felt foreign. I came from a world where we only talked about babies, food, diapers, cartoons.

That first day I felt like I didn't belong. Like I was intruding in a world that wasn't mine. At lunchtime, I locked myself in the bathroom and cried. Not out of weakness, but because the effort to stay strong had worn me out. I took a deep breath, wiped away my tears, looked at myself in the mirror and said: "This is just the first day. You don't have to know everything now. You just have to stay."

And so, I did.

I returned to my desk, observed, took notes, asked questions without shame. I learned that if I didn't know something, I could figure it out. That humility was a strength, not a weakness. And most of all, I learned that there was something inside me that held me up: a quiet force that didn't come from titles, or money, or experience. It came from my decision not to give up.

That night, when I got home, I hugged my daughters as if I hadn't seen them in a year. They were fine. Vicky had cared for them with love. And I... I had survived my first day as an independent woman.

I continued working at that company for two and a half years. Thanks to my close contact with management, I gained experience in various areas. My abilities were recognized, and I was assigned new responsibilities, which I carried out with ease and dedication. I was promoted to Buyer, also I was in charge of managing the trailer operators, becoming a key person whom they trusted—yet still earning the same salary.

I enjoyed my job, but it became urgent to increase my income. I asked for a raise and was denied. I was in debt and alone. The father of my daughters remained absent. The landlord raised the rent, and I couldn't afford to pay. My time was limited to generate enough income. I had to either pay the new rent or leave the property.

I felt a great fear of the future. I got sick. However, none of my fears came true. I found a new job within weeks, which allowed me to breathe. I learned that I needed to trust, to live in the present. I became convinced that I could solve what was essential. This time, I didn't look for a job out of fear, but with the certainty that I had the opportunity to take on a new role.

I realized I had developed a new awareness that allowed me to see how my constant choice had been to learn only through suffering. This time, I would choose a more loving way to learn.

Vision and Determination: Creating Ruhe Logistics

One day I watched a quantum physics video that talked about creating our reality. One of the scientists featured was Dr. Joe Dispenza. Later, I read his book *Breaking the Habit of Being Yourself*, which guided me to begin practicing visualization. At first, it seemed strange—how could I imagine a different future if my current reality was still so limited? But something inside me insisted. I wanted to try.

I followed Dr. Dispenza's instructions, setting my alarm to dedicating at least 15 minutes a day to practice. At first, my visualizations were very limited. But with practice, I developed my own technique. In a short time, some of my desires became reality. I began to see myself strong, confident, running a company. I visualized myself signing contracts, speaking at meetings, and leading a team. The most important thing wasn't what I saw, it was what I felt: a mix of excitement, freedom, and certainty.

I also began writing affirmations in a notebook: "I am capable," "My life is transforming," "Everything arrives at the perfect time," "I am unlimited abundance." It wasn't magic. It was a way to retrain my mind, to give myself permission to build a new version of who I was.

Another book that came into my hands was *The Power of Now* by Eckhart Tolle. It taught me to anchor myself in the present, to stop living in anguish about the future or stuck in the past. I discovered that inner peace didn't depend on everything being perfect on the outside, but on how I felt on the inside. It was a revelation. I began to practice gratitude, even for the simplest things: a quiet afternoon with my daughters, a hot meal, an encouraging message.

For the first time in years, I felt a sense of peace.

With financial stability came more energy and free time, which I used to continue my personal growth. I understood that I needed to begin living in abundance, to open my mind to new possibilities, and to believe I could achieve anything I set my mind to.

I began to clearly visualize how I wanted to feel. I let go of my fears about the future. I regained the certainty that everything would come at the right time. It was a phase where I understood something that changed everything: I didn't have to do more. It was more important to cultivate a state of being—living in peace, in abundance, with joy, with love. From there, my way of making decisions began to change. I would ask myself: "Am I choosing this out of fear or out of love?"

I dreamed bigger. I imagined myself as the director of my own company. I didn't know what kind of business it would be, or how I would achieve it. I had no money, no contacts, no business education. But I had something more powerful: absolute certainty.

One Sunday at a family gathering, when my daughters were nine years old, we were having breakfast when my Aunt Lulú asked me what I wanted to do with my life. Without hesitation, I replied: "I want to be the director of my own company."

She smiled incredulously, patted me on the back, and said mockingly: "Well, look at our little director!"

I will never forget it. Silently I told myself: "Don't listen to anyone. You know what you want." From that day on, I stopped sharing my dreams with my family. To them, it was madness. But I had already decided: I would never give up on my dreams.

Even though the vision of becoming the director of my own company was becoming clearer, I still didn't know where to start. All I had was the desire, the determination, and an idea that, although blurry, felt real inside me.

In the following years, I worked in various companies related to foreign trade and logistics. It was there that I discovered an unexpected passion: I loved the movement of goods, the processes, the planning, the organization—and most of all, the possibility of connecting countries, people, and opportunities.

I started observing carefully how logistics agencies operated: from how they treated clients to the mistakes they made that cost them money and trust. Every project, every quote, every problem became a practical class for me. I no longer worked just to earn money—I worked to learn how to build the company that would one day be mine.

If I was already doing all of this, why couldn't I do it on my own?

That's where the idea of creating RUHE Logistics was born. Ruhe means "calm" in German, and that word resonated with me. I wanted my clients to feel that: tranquility, trust, order. I wanted to create a company that was efficient, professional, and at the same time, human.

The Power of Never Giving Up

But it wasn't easy. I had no capital, no partners, no financial backing. All I had was my experience, my contacts, my reputation, and a firm certainty: I was going to make it.

I sought free advice for entrepreneurs, spoke with accountants, lawyers, and customs agents. I opened a folder labeled Ruhe and began writing down everything I needed: tax registration, a bank account, rates, suppliers, and potential clients. I had no office, so I worked from home. I used an old computer and an old phone.

I think the hardest part is letting go of the monthly paycheck. Taking that leap toward becoming an independent entrepreneur and living in uncertainty—trusting that the path will present itself—is one of the experiences that has strengthened me the most.

Today, fifteen years after that conversation, I am the CEO of RUHE Logistics, an international logistics company certified with ISO 9001.

✨ To you—woman, mother, grandmother... If you've ever felt that your dreams are impossible, I want you to know that you're not alone. I've been there too.

And if I could do it, you can do it too.

I'm here to remind you that everything you need to achieve what you dream of already exists inside you. Never give up on your dreams! Don't let anyone convince you that you can't. Yes, you can!

Chapter Two: The Half Marathon That Changed My Mind and My Life

The Longing for Something More

Have you ever felt a deep longing to achieve something, but it seemed so far away that it felt impossible? As if you didn't have the right skills, the right body, the right upbringing, the right location... as if all the circumstances were against you. That's how I felt.

I saw other people's lives as grand, and mine as just a simple succession of responsibilities. At 29, I was very young, but I already carried so much on my shoulders. I felt tired, overwhelmed, and at times disconnected from myself. I moved through the day on autopilot, fulfilling responsibilities. My body was exhausted, my thoughts overloaded, and my heart filled with fear.

It was during this stage of my life that I met a renowned holistic doctor known for helping people overcome depression, addictions, and illnesses that conventional medicine couldn't cure—without medication, only through awareness and internal work.

A Moment of Clarity: Writing Down My Dreams

During one of our sessions, he asked me a key question:—What do you want to achieve, Mónica?

He asked me to close my eyes and repeat it several times like a mantra. He handed me a yellow notebook and said:—Imagine everything is possible, that the circumstances are aligned in your favor, that you have the necessary support, the money, the knowledge, the guidance... What is it that you truly want?

I dared to write down my dreams.

It was a liberating experience. For a few minutes, I stopped feeling limited. I stopped thinking I wasn't good enough or strong enough. I let go of that constant sense of emptiness. I felt free, light, powerful. And without thinking, my hand wrote something that shook me:

"Run a half marathon."

Facing My Doubts: The Fear of The Impossible Dream

I have written it. What a huge commitment! I had never played sports in my life, not even as a child. No one in my family was athletic. I had no idea where to start. But I had already declared it. That was one of my dreams.

I was working hard at a company outside the city, and the time spent in traffic left me drained. At night I helped my daughters with homework, cooked, and went to bed very late. Every morning, I woke up with the same question: How am I going to make it through?

One day, a friend asked me: What are your dreams?

I didn't know what to answer.—I don't have time to dream, I replied.—That doesn't matter, he said. Close your eyes and imagine everything is perfect, that you have everything you need to make them come true.

I did.

And once again, I dreamed of running a race. Not to go to the Olympics, just to prove to myself that I could achieve something that seemed out of reach. That day, I realized I had been postponing my happiness out of fear, lack of time, and not knowing where to begin.

But what you don't know how to do today, you can learn tomorrow.

The First Step: Starting to Train

One day, while talking with friends, I shared this desire: I wanted to start running and someday participate in a race. One of them knew a coach and introduced us. I joined his team. I started training before work, two hours a day. My legs hurt, my body complained, but something inside me was waking up.

The first time I tried jogging; I couldn't even complete one kilometer. I felt like I was suffocating. I sat on the curb and thought, "What was I thinking? This isn't for me. But then I told myself, "What if I try one more time?" That's how it all started.

During that time, my coach would ask:—Why do you train so much if you're not committing yourself to participate in a race?

I hesitated. I was afraid. I thought I wasn't ready, that I wouldn't make it, that I already had enough stress in my life. How could something as beautiful as a dream scare me so much?

Embracing the Struggle: Becoming a Runner

But I kept training. My daughters saw me leave early, in my old sneakers with a water bottle. Sometimes they would ask if I was already a professional runner. I smiled and told them, "Not yet, but I'm learning." Without knowing it, they were learning from my example. They saw me fall, get up, and persist. And that, more than any medal, was valuable.

Until one day, I woke up and simply decided: I'm going to run this half marathon. It doesn't matter how long it takes—I will finish. I'll run at my own speed.

Just deciding was transformative. My body responded, my mind aligned. I felt ready.

Crossing the Line: More Than Just a Race

The day before the half marathon, the team had a ritual of going out for pasta dinner, since the energy it provided was needed to endure the race. The next morning, I woke up very early, before the sun was out. I felt somewhat calm because I would meet my team and we'd walk together to the starting point. I put on my team shirt with my race number and my favorite sneakers.

It's such an emotional experience to be at the starting line with all the runners gathered, waiting for the signal to begin.

During the race, I experienced all kinds of emotions. I believe a race is lived the way you live your life. There were moments of euphoria when ego took over, moments of deep connection with my body and with life. But there were also moments of extreme exhaustion, doubt, and the urge to give up. Part of me was screaming, "Stop! This is too much," and I cried. But a stronger part replied, "Keep going. You're closer than you think."

My daughters were waiting for me at the most difficult part of the route. I had asked them to be there on purpose—it was several kilometers of steep incline. I cried before reaching them, I couldn't go on, but I couldn't give up because they were waiting. As soon as I saw them, they shouted, "Go, Mom! You can do it!" Their support gave me so much strength.

I remembered all the times I thought I couldn't. I remembered the yellow notebook, the late nights, the tears, the doubts.

And I kept running.

I crossed the finish line.

And with it, I crossed a mental barrier that had followed me my entire life.

I felt an indescribable energy—a mix of pride, gratitude, and joy. I hugged myself like never before.

That half marathon wasn't just a physical race. It was a race against my fears, my mental limits, and my own beliefs.

A New Beginning: Trusting Myself and My Dreams

Today I know it wasn't just a sporting event. It was an initiation. A rebirth.

From that point on, everything changed. I started trusting myself more. Making decisions from certainty, no doubt. Looking at my daughters with more strength and telling them from the bottom of my heart: "You can do anything you set your mind to."

If you also have a dream that feels impossible, I want to tell you something: Never stop trying. Even if today, you don't know how to do it, start by dreaming about it. Then take the first step.

And trust yourself. Because if I could do it, you can do it too.

Chapter Three: Earning Respect as a Female Leader from Humble Beginnings

Starting from Scratch: The Struggle of a Single Mother
I was 29 years old and had been working for two and a half years in my first job as an executive assistant. I earned just enough to cover the basics: the nanny's salary, diapers, baby formula, food, gas, and medical expenses. I couldn't afford my rent. The landlord knew that my ex-husband had only paid the first month and then disappeared. For over two years, he didn't pay a single peso more. Although the landlord had compassion for me and my two babies, he also wanted to recover his money with interest. The situation had become unsustainable. I urgently needed a better-paying job.

As we did every Saturday, we were gathered as a family when my uncle Lalo handed me a newspaper with a job listings section. There was a vacancy at a large mining corporation. I applied. I went to two interviews, and, in less than four days, I was hired.

It was a huge company, over 30 years old. Everything there was traditional and rigid—almost like a mammoth. All the executives were men, engineers with years of experience. How was I, a young woman with an accounting background and little experience, supposed to survive as head of the purchasing department at a mining plant? On top of that, the last few purchasing managers have all been fired before completing two years.

Fighting for Respect: Dismissal and Frustration
My first challenge was to participate in the Monday meetings, where the most relevant operational topics were discussed. Every time I raised my hand to speak, my boss would say:—Please don't speak. You have no idea what we're talking about.

I went home crying out of frustration. I kept asking myself: How am I going to earn the respect of my boss and all these managers?

I couldn't give up. I armed myself with patience and dedicated myself to doing my job the best I could. I had the enormous responsibility of negotiating with suppliers and contractors to keep the plant running 24/7 all year long.

I got up at 4 a.m. to study purchasing policies. On weekends, I learned about international trade and customs operations. I thoroughly analyzed the purchasing processes. I began making improvements: eliminated unnecessary administrative tasks, integrated the purchasing department into the ERP system, and trained the staff to use it. I incorporated all these changes into the ISO 9001 system, corrected existing procedures, and adapted them to our operations and objectives. I identified the highest spending categories and optimized annual negotiations with suppliers, which reduced operational costs and increased the commitment of our business partners.

Standing Firm: Challenging Authority

One Monday during a meeting, an expansion project was presented to double production capacity. The project manager had already requested quotes but didn't include me in the process. My boss handed me a package with three supplier proposals and instructed me which one to hire, by passing corporate purchasing policies.

There was a policy called "Assigned Supplier," in which three quotes weren't required for comparison, but a memorandum signed by the operations director was necessary to authorize the decision. Since my position was closely monitored by both the local and international corporate controllers, I asked my boss to provide the memorandum. And he did.

Meanwhile, I analyzed all the proposals, researched the suppliers, their experience, locations, and the brands of equipment they offered. I asked my boss for a meeting to present my observations:

1. The selected supplier's infrastructure didn't guarantee the project would be completed on time or within budget.
2. There were significant discrepancies between the three technical proposals.
3. There was no guaranteed access to replacement parts or maintenance services for the suggested equipment, which posed an operational risk.

I suggested we review everything before making a final decision.

My boss insisted:—Just do what I'm asking you to do!

I replied:—I'll do it, but if something goes wrong, don't ask me to fix it. That will be the project manager's job.

He agreed.

Gaining Respect: From Ignored to Trusted Leader

A month later, the problems started. Everything I warned about happened. The project was delayed, costs had skyrocketed, and my boss had to give explanations to the board of directors in the U.S.

The Project Manager couldn't resolve the situation and couldn't handle the pressure. My boss had no choice but to ask me for help.

He came into my office, overwhelmed, and asked for my help.

I said yes. I told him I would solve it.

I called in the supplier's legal representative and informed him we would cancel the contract due to non-compliance, demanding the corresponding penalties. I immediately hired the supplier I had originally recommended. Although the situation was tense, the new company was professional and successfully completed the project.

The following Monday, during the general meeting, my boss announced: "From today onward, every purchase made in the company, including new projects, must be reviewed by Mónica. She will make the final decision on what is best for the company."

That day marked a turning point. Finally, after three years of tireless work, I felt that my voice had weight, that my decisions were respected, that my constant effort was paying off. I had not only earned the respect of my boss but of the entire organization. But beyond the formal recognition, what truly transformed me was the journey I took to reach that point—full of silent sacrifices, internal doubts, and deep solitude.

From the outside, many thought I was just lucky. What they didn't know was how many times I worked until dawn, how many weekends I spent locked up studying, or that while fulfilling my professional duties, I had also returned to university to study for a master's in international business. It was a demanding, intense, and exhausting phase. But also, a deeply formative one. There were many nights when I cried silently, after my daughters were asleep, when the physical and emotional exhaustion overwhelmed me. Being a young single mother, without a solid support network and with two small children in my care, was already a huge challenge. But to also be a woman determined to stand out in a male-dominated work environment was a daily battle.

Entrepreneurship: From Employee to Founder of RUHE Logistics

One of the hardest things was learning not to doubt myself when others did. There were those who looked at me with disdain, who questioned every decision I made—not because of a lack of reasoning, but simply because I was a woman. Some corrected me in public trying to embarrass me; others waited for any mistake to point out with sarcasm. At first, that hurt deeply. But over time, I understood that the best way to respond was not with confrontation, but with results.

I became a woman of data, of solid arguments, of impeccable presentations. I learned to anticipate conflicts, to read team dynamics, to prepare with such attention to detail that I felt secure even in the most demanding scenarios.

I realized that it wasn't enough to do my job well—I had to do it exceptionally well. I began building trusting relationships with suppliers—not through imposition, but through transparency. I kept my promises, negotiated firmly but respectfully, and that created lasting alliances that strengthened my position.

Over time, my opinion began to be valued. I was invited to meetings where I was previously not even considered. Even some of the engineers who had initially doubted me began to ask how I had done it. I always gave the same answer: by working harder than anyone else, preparing as if every day were a test, and believing in myself when no one else did.

I worked at that company for five years. It was my school, my battlefield, my springboard. But at the end of that cycle, I began to feel a growing restlessness: I wanted to move into sales. They said that if you were a good buyer, you could be an even better seller, but the change scared me. A fear common among employees—the fear of losing the secure paycheck every two weeks.

And yet, life gave me the push I needed. One day, without further explanation, I was let go. My time at that company had come to an end. At first, I felt dizzy. But soon, that uncertainty turned into momentum. I sent my resume to several companies and almost immediately received an offer to join the sales department of a food company. I was thrilled—but also scared. I knew my duties would be completely different, and to be honest, I didn't know if I was ready.

The biggest change was that now I had to be out in the field. As a buyer, I waited for suppliers to visit me in my office. Now, I had to go find them, knock on doors, make cold calls, and organize visit routes. I learned to manage my time, set daily goals, and most importantly, to understand that selling wasn't just offering a product, but creating a connection with the client. And to my surprise, it wasn't as hard as I had imagined. Within a few months, that job stopped being a challenge, and I began to crave new ones.

After nine months, I left that company. From that point on, I never searched for another job again—companies started reaching out to me. My reputation in the industry was beginning to grow.

Later, I was hired as Regional Sales Manager by a leading international transportation company. I stayed there for six years. It was a key stage in my career: I received deep training in cargo movement, packaging, security, international law compliance... and built a solid client portfolio. My name was starting to carry weight in the sector. I became known for being firm, professional, and committed. That reputation opened many doors and, more importantly, made me realize that I had what it took to go further.

My last job was at a small logistics company. They only had five trucks, a very limited client portfolio, and were far from profitable. They hired me as Sales

Manager and from day one I saw all the potential that could be developed there. I implemented a commercial strategy to keep the trucks constantly running, expanded the types of operations, and began to build a solid network of reliable suppliers: transport, insurance, courier, maritime services.

Additionally, I developed a basic work system, training the operations and administrative staff. We organized the processes, established controls, strengthened customer relationships, and raised the level of professionalism of the entire operation. I stayed there for five years. It was like creating a company... only for someone else.

And then came the question I could no longer ignore: Why, if I was practically doing everything a business owner does, wasn't I taking the next step and starting my own company?

I didn't do it right away. I was held back by a value I still consider fundamental: loyalty. I didn't want to harm the owner of the company by taking his clients. It seemed unfair, and I wasn't going to betray my principles. But fate once again opened the door for me. A year later, the majority of partner decided to shut down the company to focus on other investments. Then everything changed.

The clients, far from drifting away, came looking for me. They told me they trusted me, that they wanted to continue working with me. And so, with all the experience I had accumulated, with all the lessons, with all the fears and all the determination, I founded my own company: RUHE Logistics.

I understood that respect is not demanded, it is earned. And I earned it through work, preparation, and courage.

Never give up. Never doubt your ability to rewrite your story. Because if I could do it, so can you.

Author's BIO
Monica Arce
Founder & CEO- Ruhe Logistics, Mexico

Monica Arce is the Founder and CEO of **Ruhe Logistics**, a pioneering global logistics company based in Mexico. As a dynamic leader, Monica is not only renowned for her strategic vision and business acumen but also for her unwavering commitment to mentoring and empowering the next generation of leaders, particularly in Spanish-speaking countries.

A respected force in the logistics industry, Monica has built a reputation as a visionary entrepreneur and a dedicated mentor to younger professionals aspiring to succeed in business. She has worked tirelessly to foster a culture of growth and innovation, driving her company's success while also coaching emerging leaders and entrepreneurs to unlock their full potential.

Monica's leadership style is rooted in authenticity, transparency, and empowerment. Her ability to mentor young professionals and encourage them to take bold steps toward their goals is what truly sets her apart. Known for her independence and adaptability, she champions change and embraces new opportunities with an open mind, helping others to do the same.

In her personal life, Monica is an advocate for balance and well-being, practicing yoga, reading, and exploring culinary arts. She deeply values time with her loved ones and is especially close to her independent and vibrant twin daughters, Michelle and Marcela, who live near her in Guadalajara, Mexico.

Linkedin: https://www.linkedin.com/in/monica-arce-856565212/

Chapter 8

From Struggles to Success Kalana Wickramaratne's Journey in Logistics

Kalana Wickramaratne

"My life has been like a river—sometimes calm and steady, other times turbulent and unpredictable, but always moving forward."

A Life Shaped by Family, Values, and Struggle

My story begins in a very quite and family oriented back ground where my father used to held a very good position in a very strong NGO company in the country. Born into a family that had everything from Vehicles / servants / money and lot of love. I grew up without knowing the harsh realities of life. My parents, though financially stable, also were rich in values. They believed in hard work, honesty, and resilience their qualities that would later shape my character.

I was born in 1981 February 24th in Colombo. Later when I search what are the important events that happened on by birthday and I found out that British Queen Diana and Charles had got married on that day. That's the only thing I can remember and after that I never look for any thing as such. By the way I have 1 smaller brother and now he is living in Canada with the Family. My mother was a house wife who sacrified her line for both mine and my brothers education.

To continue our Wickramaratne family legacy my father send us to the same school which he studied. Nalanda College where everything created for me and I must thanks my mother Nalanda for shaping me to be who I'm today. So I was the second generation of Wickramaratne family to study at Nalanda College. Legary continue and after that I managed to send my son also to Nalanda College. If I don't say anything about my school Nalanda it will be a vacume in this story. Nalanda College is the only Buddhist School in Colombo which is well renowned as one of the best schools in Sri Lanka. If you can't identify the school, what I can say is that it's the school which has produced great Scinetist / Lawyers / Doctor / Politicial / Businesman and sportsmen to the country. To Calrify more It's the school who produced great cricketers such as Roshan Mahanama / Asanka Gurusinghe and Mahela Jayawardena.

During the school time I was a Prefect. As far i know i was one of the few who has held the Prefect position in school for longest time. Out of my 13 year time in school I was a prefect for 8 years continuously. I managed to do my studding well and also perform well at inter school level in 400m running. I belive that Athlatices, Specially 400m event thought me many things such as to face win or loose and be humble at every situation. Also gave me the courage to face any obstacle in life.

The Turbulence of Adversity: From Comfort to Hardship

When I was in grade 4 my father lost his job and we had to move from luxurius Colombo city to out of Colombo a place call Halpita. Which is located in Kesbewa polling division. When we are moving there there was no Electriity / Telephone.

So here came the first turbulence in my life.........

My father fail to find a job and he was short of money. But I remember my father use to take us to school by moter bike. Both my self and my brother. We never missed any school day and even during the rainy days my father took us to the school.

As I told earlier I did my studies well and managed to get through with Grade 5 scholarship with 151 marks which was a good mark at that time. Got through the ordinary level exam with very good grades and finally advance level AL's in year 2000. I was fortunate to leave the school as a member of Millenium Batch.

The family's struggles were a constant reminder of the challenges we faced. I often recalls the cold nights when our family couldn't afford proper meals and the countless times my parents sacrificed their needs for the sake of me and my brother. These moments instilled in me a sense of responsibility and a burning desire to rise above my circumstances.

My childhood was marked by resilience. The poverty I experienced gave me a unique perspective on life, teaching me to appreciate small victories and to stay grounded. I often says, *"My roots are my strength. They remind me of where I come from and keep me focused on where I want to go."* My early struggles became the foundation of my empathy and determination, qualities that would later define my leadership.

From Rejection to Redemption: A Career Built on Perseverance

As a young adult, i faced what seemed like an endless series of setbacks. Graduating with dreams of a brighter future, I found my self in a job market that offered little to someone from my background. Job applications were met with rejections; interviews ended in disappointment. This period of his life was a cycle of hope and despair.

The financial strain on my family only added to the pressure. I vividly remembers the nights i spent questioning my worth, wondering if I would ever be able to provide a better life for those I loved. Despite the darkness, i found solace in my determination to keep trying.

"I ran through the crowded streets, clutching the letter that would change my life forever. The words burned in my mind: 'We regret to inform you...'"

I though I would get an opportunity at a bank since I was a good Athlete. Can remember I went till final Interview at HSBC bank and got rejected. Also almost got selected as a Athletic Coach at a leading International School and finally didn't get appointed since I was too young. During this time my father did physiotherapy for a Dutch gentleman in Colombo. He has given my CV to his son Mr. Thomas Gerlash who had his company call Sailaani Exports which was a Coir Fiber Export company. Since I was at home he wanted me to come and meet him. So I met him and he offered me a job as a Management Trainee at the company. My starting Salary was LKR 4000/= per month in year 2001.

With the oppurtunity I got I learn all the areas of that company and I handle the petty cash / Did the Balance sheet / prepared the Export documents / learned to check the quality / Did the factory visit. So with in short period of time I became a all rounder.

With the financial situation of the family I missed to continue with the studies. But some how I managed to pay the class fees and got my self enrol to do the CIM. (Charted Institute of Marketing) I lean well. But I didn't has enough money to pay for the UK exam fees. So I had to give up the exam. But I carried out my learnings from the classes. With Never give us attitude again got enroll for the 2nd stage of the CIM hoping to get through both the stages together. I requested a loan from the company. Unfortunately got rejected. So again had to give up on the exams and I carried away only with the learings. No certificates.

While working at Sailaani I learn lot of basics and aspects in export documents and logistics. I likes it and most importantly I enjoyed it. So I thought of further study in Logistics and got enrolled to Charted Shipbroking. I really enjoyed it.

The Accident That Changed Everything

Amid my struggles, i faced a life-altering accident. The physical pain was immense, but the emotional toll was even heavier. Unable to work, I felt like i was failing not just myself but my family. Depression loomed over me, and i began to question my path.

Yet, it was during this time of despair that i discovered an invaluable lesson: honesty. I realized that being truthful—with myself and with others—was the key to rebuilding my life. This newfound clarity became my guiding principle.

Lessons Learned

My journey through pain taught me resilience, the importance of self-belief, and the value of honesty.I shares, *"It's not the fall that defines you, but how you rise again. Every setback is an opportunity to grow."*

With the accident my lost my left hand middle finger. Has to stay in the bed for over a month. When I return to work Mr. Thomas has sold the company and I had to face the new management and they want me to keep on riding the motor cycle which I refused. So had to leave the company after 2+ years.

Again went searching for job opportunities. I started sending application for logistics companies based on the little experience that I had and with little knowledge I gain. Sorry I missed to sit for the Shipbrokering exam due to the accident. But I took away the knowledge.

Turner round in life again…Didn't understand how this universe treat the people…

"Life has a way of teaching you the greatest lessons when you least expect them, and for me, it came in the form of losing everything I thought I needed."

After many application I was fortunate to call for interview from two companies. One is from Mr. Thomas's New company Malwatte Wally Plantation as State Suparindent. Other one from Maritime Agencies currently known as Hayleys Advantis. Two interviews on same day same time. I had a choise to make….

My Love….My first Love…Madhusha. We are now blessed with 2 children and happy married for 17 years. I met my love at Dhamma School when we are in grade 10. Both were at the same class. She also came from one of the best Girls Schools in the country. It was Vishaka Vidyalaya. She was behind be all the time. I remember one time I couldn't get the money for track kit for Atlatic meet due to the financial issues we had at home. She got to know this and gave me the money for that and still I don't know who she arranged it. Also she was the first one to came to see me at the hospital when I met with the accident and even though I lost my job and finger she didn't give up on me. So I reached to her and ask her opinion for which interview to go. She asked me to go for the interview at the Maritime Agencies. After 3 round of Interview and one exam had to go for one last interview with Mr. Mohan Pandithage who is currently the Chairmen for Hayles PLC. One of the most trusted blue chip company in Sri Lanka. I went to the interview with the stiched in my lost finger. I got a form to fill and there was a question to mention about the physical condition of the applicant. I always remember my learning and being honest I wrote the truth. My Pandithage aske me his usual famous 3 questions and I gave the honest answers to those says "YES".After that he aske about the finger and I told the story and I was fortunate to get selected. He had auspicious days for new comers to join and he wants me to start working from next Thursday. From that day onwards I also start believing Thursday as a auspicious day.

In 4 th April 2003 I Join Maritime Agencies as a Cleark. My starting Salary was LKR 7500/- and I was entitled for OT. Management Traineed to Cleark. I trusted my self and started my carrier at Hayles Advantis and learn most aspected and every single thing in logistics. I appointment was subject to 6 months probation. Them only the company confirm based on your work performance. But I was fortunate to get promoted as Junior Excutive when I completed by 6 month probation. I think I'm the only one. In 2006 not the oppurtunity to work as a Sales Executive. I gave this oppurtunity after requesting the management for it for 3 time. Every time they said no and recruited and new one from outside. Good thing is that before asking for sales and while I was working as a sales coordinator I prepared my self doing my tele sales. On the day I got the my First vehicle I managed to close 3 new accounts.

With long stand of 13+ years from Cleark I climbed the corporate ladder and became a Manager at Hayleys Advantis. It was a interesting and challenging journey at ADV. Luckily I had two great bosses. One is Mohan Fernando who gave me the opportunity to lean all. Other one is Ranil Polonowita who guided me and encourage me.

Some time being honest and telling the truth became a dis advantage for me. So due to my straightness and openness most of the other Managers and company heads who came after Ranil didn't line me. But I managed to keep my head up swim though the rough. By being my self I believed I did my very best for the company and I know still most of them know that and talk about it.

The Rise of Ocean 7: Building a Legacy in Logistics
After working for 13 + Yeasr becoming a Manager and heading the Export department I felt that I'm getting stuck at my position for aa long time. So I decided to look out for opportunities out side. But this time with good quality experience / Proven track record and very good reputation with in the

industry. Most of the companies wanted me to join as a Sales Manger with higher package. I refused. I had confident in my capabilities and I was exactly knew what I was doing. When I got call by the C.H. Robinson I met them and discuss and they offered me the same Sales Manager position which I refused and told them I'm in the sales Manager position and was in the management team of the company. After few days they offered me a job as a Country Manger at C.H. Robinson, Sri Lanka. Hope all know what C.H. Robinson is. It's the fortune 100 companies in USA and one of the top 5 logistics companies in the world.

My perseverance began to pay off when i joined C.H. Robinson. Starting at the bottom, i poured my heart and soul into my work. my innovative ideas and relentless work ethic didn't go unnoticed. Over time, he climbed the corporate ladder, eventually becoming a Director at CHR Sri Lanka.

Under my leadership, the company flourished. I implemented strategies that transformed operations, drove growth, and positioned C.H. Robinson as a leader in the market. My achievements earned me widespread recognition and respect.

Lessons of Leadership: Integrity, Empathy, and Resilience

However, life threw another curveball. With changes in the top management team, I found my falling from the top of the mountain I had worked so hard to climb. It was a humbling experience, one that tested my resilience once again.

I reflects, *"Success isn't permanent, and failure isn't fatal. What matters is the courage to continue."* This period of my life was a reminder that even in the face of adversity, it's possible to rebuild.

This time looking for opportunities were little difficult as coming out as top level person and finding a suitable position was challenging. Went for few interviews but all were looking for a Sales Manager position. During time time I worked as a Taxi driver through Uber app.

One day I met this wonderful person Kolitha Wickramasinge who was well known industry export / leader. We have worked together but never had any close connection. So I approached him for a job opportunity. We had a very interesting conversation and at the end he told me "kalana, You're a brand in the market. Why don't you start your own company and I will send you" These words went deep in to my mind and I came home with this idea.

At this time only I realised who are ready good friends are since I have help so many people and there was no on to guide me and helped me during this time. But I felt Kolitha was great in that was and being a super human being.

He would have easily hired me for his company but instead he encourage me to move in to different task..

After long thinking I decided to start my own company. I has only very little money and move ahead with it. I wanted to have a company name that can go in to international market. So with lot of discussion with my wife I came up with name as "OCEAN 7 Logistics (Pvt) Ltd" Now after many years I realize and many have told me that OCEAN 7 is very strong and meaningful name and now it has become a brand.

I would like say few things about the company logo. This came to my mind as I told earlier that I was a good athlete and Olympic logo was in my mind. After thinking lot I realised that OCEAN name can easily fit in to as Olympic logo. Recently at a conference few of them told me that OCEAN 7 logo is the most interesting logo that they have seen and they likes it lot.

Determined to take control of my destiny, I decided to start my own company. The journey was far from easy. I reached out to people i had helped in the past, only to find that few were willing to return the favor. This rejection fueled my determination.

Through sheer grit and unwavering focus, I built my company from the ground up. Today, it stands as a testament to my vision and hard work. The company has not only achieved financial success but has also earned numerous awards and recognition for its contributions to the industry.

One of my proudest achievements is my work with young professionals. I have made it my mission to mentor and train the next generation, offering them opportunities that i once struggled to find. My passion for the logistics industry and my commitment to people are at the heart of everything i do.

"Success is meaningful when it's shared. I want to create a ripple effect, empowering others to achieve their dreams."

My love for the logistics industry goes beyond business. I see it as a platform to create meaningful change, to connect people and opportunities, and to drive progress. My vision is to help more business owners navigate the challenges of the industry and achieve sustainable success.

My journey is a beacon of hope for those facing adversity. I want readers to know that no matter where they start, it's possible to rise above challenges and achieve greatness. My message is simple: *"Believe in yourself, stay honest, and never give up."*

Through my experiences, I have learned invaluable lessons about leadership:
- The importance of empathy and understanding.
- The value of honesty and integrity.
- The power of resilience and perseverance.

These lessons are not just for business leaders but for anyone striving to make a difference in their lives and the lives of others.

My story is one of resilience, determination, and transformation. From a humble beginning to the heights of success, and from the depths of despair to building my own legacy, my journey is an inspiration to all. my life is a testament to the power of belief, the importance of honesty, and the impact of perseverance.

In 2024 I was privileged to win the **Under 45 Global CEO Platinum Award for Leadership Excellence** Recognized for outstanding leadership in driving business success and organizational growth as the only person from logistics industry in Sri Lanka.

Also won few recognitions few leading global logistics network as the best partner in Sri Lanka.

My message to readers is clear: *"Your past does not define your future. Embrace your journey, learn from your struggles, and never lose sight of your dreams."*

OCEAN 7 Logistics (Pvt) Ltd…." We freight relationships"

Author's BIO
Kalana Wickramaratne
Founder & CEO, Ocean 7 Logistics (Pvt) Ltd.

With over 15 years of leadership experience in the international logistics and supply chain management industry, Kalana Wickramaratne has established himself as a prominent figure in the logistics sector, known for his strategic foresight, operational excellence, and ability to drive growth. Throughout his career, Kalana has been at the helm of numerous high-performing teams, leading them to deliver exceptional results across multiple international markets.

Kalana's career began at **Hayleys Advantis Limited**, where he gained extensive experience across various sales, marketing, and operational roles. His deep understanding of international trade, rate negotiations, and supply chain management led him to a pivotal role as Branch Manager at **C.H. Robinson Freight Services Lanka**, where he successfully managed operations, sales, and profitability, positioning the branch for long-term success.

In 2017, Kalana took a bold step in entrepreneurship, founding **Ocean 7 Logistics (Pvt) Ltd.**, with a clear vision to create a global logistics company that would provide customized, cutting-edge solutions to clients worldwide. Under his leadership, Ocean 7 has grown rapidly, gaining recognition for its innovation, customer-centric approach, and operational efficiency.

Kalana's leadership philosophy is cantered on **integrity**, **empathy**, and **resilience**. His commitment to fostering sustainable business practices and building long-term relationships with stakeholders has earned him industry-wide recognition. Notably, he was awarded the **Under 45 Global CEO Platinum Award for Leadership Excellence**, a testament to his exceptional ability to drive organizational growth and inspire his teams.

A forward-thinking leader, Kalana continues to push the boundaries of the logistics industry, mentoring the next generation of professionals and contributing to the development of best practices in global supply chain management.

LinkedIn: https://www.linkedin.com/in/kalana-wickramaratne-b9348113b/

Let's Connect

If you are interested to be the next co-author in the next book, register and apply here:
https://kristyguo.com/signature-influencer-author-program/

Or go to www.kristyguo.com

Join the World's Thought Leaders Movement!

Have you ever considered sharing your **leadership story** with the world? Do you believe your insights and experiences could inspire others to lead with greater impact?

The Logistics Legends isn't just a book, it's a **global movement** of visionary leaders who are shaping the future through their stories, wisdom, and influence.

Are You Ready to:

☑ Be recognized as a global thought leader?
☑ Share your leadership journey in an upcoming volume?
☑ Connect with an exclusive community of high-impact leaders?

💡 **Your Voice Matters. Your Story Deserves to Be Heard.**
✉ **Join the World's Thought Leader & Logistics Legends Global Community Today!**

Email **cuilanguo@outlook.com** and take the first step toward inspiring the world with your leadership and logistics legendary journey.

Your leadership legacy starts here!

Connect with Kristy by scanning the code above

Connect with SGN by scanning the code above

Powered by

Books Also by Cuilan Guo (Kristy)

The last Two Co-Authors Book Signing Ceremony

The left Pic– The Logistics Legends Volume 1: co-authors: from the left to the right: Kristy, Deepanker, Gilbert, Sri, Rudee, Mandy

The Right Pic- The World's Thought Leaders: co-authors: from the left to the right: Peter Sundara, Justus Kluver-Schlotfeldt, Cassie Gruber, Kristy Guo, Simon De Raadt, Douglas Gozmao, Victor Hermosa, Leslie Swamy

www.ingramcontent.com/pod-product-compliance
Lightning Source LLC
Chambersburg PA
CBHW072000290426
44109CB00018B/2087